W9-BRD-573

Nick Harrison is a man of the Word, the Word God promises won't return void, that will accomplish his purposes, that is the power of God unto salvation. There is something living and dynamic about the Word, and Nick taps into it, fashioning it into daily prayers that can change a life and infuse it with power. I don't know about you, but that's an offer I can't pass up.

Jerry B. Jenkins, novelist and biographer; owner, Christian Writers Guild

I confess I'm a Nick Harrison fan. His previous work, *Magnificent Prayer*, is a daily dose of divine perspective in my life, and I can't imagine anyone will be disappointed by his latest, *Power in the Promises*.

Chip Ingram, senior pastor, Venture Christian Church; president, Living on the Edge; author, True Spirituality, Good to Great in God's Eyes, *and* The Invisible War

Nick Harrison's *Power in the Promises* is a great reminder that a life built on the promises of God is a life that cannot fail.

Dr. Tony Evans, senior pastor, Oak Cliff Bible Fellowship; author, Victory in Spiritual Warfare *and* Kingdom Man

Open these pages and you will be transformed! God's goodness to us radiates through his promises. You will experience renewed hope and joy as you discover afresh his unconditional love for you.

Glenna Salsbury, author, Heavenly Treasures, More Heavenly Treasures, *and* The Art of the Fresh Start

God's promises are the believer's birthright, but how easily they're neglected or forgotten! Nick Harrison serves them up afresh in this terrific catalogue of divine assurances, arranged so everyone can easily match their current need to just the right promise. To read *Power in the Promises* is to be refreshed and built up.

Joe Dallas, author, The Game Plan and Desires in Conflict

Nick Harrison wants us to face the roughest moments of life with God's promises on our lips and faith in our hearts. You will find *Power in the Promises* to be a unique blessing and useful tool for staying strong in the Lord.

Jim Cymbala, pastor, The Brooklyn Tabernacle

One of our finest contemporary devotional writers, Nick Harrison now gives us a powerful and transforming work based on the promises and affirmations of Scripture. You cannot read *Power in the Promises* even once without experiencing a new joy and excitement in your life journey as you learn to anchor your faith on God's Word—and discover that the anchor does indeed hold.

> *B. J. Hoff, author,* The American Anthem Series
> *and* The Emerald Ballad Series

Nick Harrison writes with clarity, passion, and commitment about something that affects everyone: Is God going to be there for us during the difficult passages of life? And his answer is a resounding yes, the God who loves us and gave himself for us has promised not only to stand by his word, but stand by us, come what may. This is that great sort of book that heals the broken spirit and puts the heart back in men and women of faith.

> *Murray Pura, pastor; author,* Rooted, Streams, *and* Majestic and Wild

Like Nick Harrison, we have seen the power of Scripture to transform, redeem, and empower a life. Nick has made it so easy to apply God's Word to real life, making *Power in the Promises* a must-have for every person who wants the best God desires for his or her life.

> *Pam and Bill Farrel, authors,* A Couple's Journey with God *and*
> Men Are Like Waffles, Women Are Like Spaghetti *and 36 others*

POWER IN THE PROMISES

PRAYING GOD'S WORD TO CHANGE YOUR LIFE

NICK HARRISON

ZONDERVAN®

We want to hear from you. Please send your comments about this
book to us in care of zreview@zondervan.com. Thank you.

ZONDERVAN

Power in the Promises

Copyright © 2013 by Nick Harrison

This title is also available as a Zondervan ebook. Visit www.zondervan.com/ebooks.

Requests for information should be addressed to:

Zondervan, *Grand Rapids, Michigan* 49530

Library of Congress Cataloging-in-Publication Data

Harrison, Nick.
    Power in the promises : praying God's word to change your life / Nick Harrison. — 1st [edition].
      pages cm
    Includes bibliographical references and index [if applicable].
    ISBN 978-0-310-33721-8 (softcover)
    1. Bible—Indexes. 2. Bible—Devotional use. 3. Self-talk—Religious aspects—Christianity. I. Title.
    BS432.H29 2013
    242'.5—dc23
                                                   2013035592

Unless otherwise indicated, Scripture quotations are taken from the Holy Bible, *New International Version*®, *NIV*®. Copyright © 1973, 1978, 1984, 2011 by Biblica, Inc.® Used by permission. All rights reserved worldwide.

Scripture quotations marked AMP are taken from the Amplified® Bible, copyright © 1954, 1958, 1962, 1964, 1965, 1987 by The Lockman Foundation. Used by permission.

Scripture quotations marked ESV are taken from The Holy Bible, English Standard Version® (ESV®), copyright © 2001 by Crossway, a publishing ministry of Good News Publishers. Used by permission. All rights reserved. ESV Text Edition: 2007.

Scripture quotations marked KJV are taken from the King James Version of the Bible. Scripture quotations marked MSG are from *THE MESSAGE*. Copyright © by Eugene H. Peterson 1993, 1994, 1995, 1996, 2000, 2001, 2002. Used by permission of NavPress Publishing Group.

Scripture quotations marked NKJV are taken from the New King James Version. Copyright © 1982 by Thomas Nelson, Inc. Used by permission. All rights reserved.

Scripture quotations marked NRSV are taken from the *New Revised Standard Version of the Bible*, copyrighted 1989 by the Division of Christian Education of the National Council of Churches of Christ in the United States of America, and are used by permission. All rights reserved.

I'm a lover of good quotes, as readers of my previous books can attest to. To find these gems, I scour a lot of books and websites, many of which don't always offer a citation of which of the author's books is being quoted. One of the best sites I've found for quotes is www.ochristian.com. If you enjoy the many quotes in *Power in the Promises* I think you'll want to visit this useful site. —Nick Harrison

Any Internet addresses (websites, blogs, etc.) and telephone numbers printed in this book are offered as a resource. They are not intended in any way to be or imply an endorsement by Zondervan, nor does Zondervan vouch for the content of these sites and numbers for the life of this book.

All rights reserved. No part of this publication may be reproduced, stored in a retrieval system, or transmitted in any form or by any means — electronic, mechanical, photocopy, recording, or any other — except for brief quotations in printed reviews, without the prior permission of the publisher.

Published in association with Kimberly Shumate of the Living Word Literary Agency.

Cover photograph: James Randklev/Getty Images®
Interior design and composition: Greg Johnson/Textbook Perfect

Printed in the United States of America

---

13 14 15 16 17 18 /DCI/ 22 21 20 19 18 17 16 15 14 13 12 11 10 9 8 7 6 5 4 3 2 1

This is for Beverly,
the one true love of my life.

And now, Lord God, keep forever the promise you have made concerning your servant and his house. Do as you promised.

2 SAM. 7:25

Not one word has failed of all [the Lord's] good promises.

1 KINGS 8:56

For no word from God will ever fail.

LUKE 1:37

For no matter how many promises God has made, they are "Yes" in Christ.

2 COR. 1:20

He who promised is faithful.

HEB. 10:23

CONTENTS

ACKNOWLEDGMENTS

I'd like to acknowledge several people who have impacted my life down through the years: Noni Noble, one of the first Christians I knew who showed forth Christ — and still does; Elaine Wright Colvin, a wonderful cheerleader for my writing career for many years; Jan Brophy, a man who understands the power of God's Word; and Cec Murphey, truly one of the great encouragers in my life. My life has been made better by your friendship.

My brothers and sisters in Christ at Willamette Bible Chapel have been a blessing to me for several years now. Thank you for your enthusiasm for standing on the promises of God.

Much thanks to the good folks at Zondervan, including Carolyn McCready, Bob Hudson, and Laura Weller.

Thanks also to Kimberly Shumate for your long-term belief in me.

And, of course, my family; God's greatest earthly gift to me. *Thank you.*

PART 1

WHAT IS SELF-TALK FROM THE BIBLE?

God never made a promise too good to be true.

D. L. MOODY

Here's a question for you: Are Christians supposed to live happy, trouble-free lives?

Okay, wait. I confess, it's a trick question. The answer is yes and no. *Yes*, the Christian should always be happy, but *no*, the Christian life will not always be trouble-free. I'm sure you agree with the last part of my answer, but I'm guessing you're not so sure about the "always happy" part.

Still, the Bible — the source of truth for Christians — confirms both answers in several places. Here are some verses about trouble:

- The LORD is a refuge for the oppressed, a stronghold in times of trouble. (Ps. 9:9)

- For in the day of trouble he will keep me safe in his dwelling; he will hide me in the shelter of his sacred tent and set me high upon a rock. (Ps. 27:5)

- You are my hiding place; you will protect me from trouble and surround me with songs of deliverance. (Ps. 32:7)

- This poor man called, and the LORD heard him; he saved him out of all his troubles. (Ps. 34:6)

- The righteous person may have many troubles, but the LORD delivers him from them all. (Ps. 34:19)

- The LORD is good, a refuge in times of trouble. He cares for those who trust in him. (Nah. 1:7)

- Praise be to the God and Father of our Lord Jesus Christ, the Father of compassion and the God of all comfort, who comforts us in all our troubles, so that we can comfort those in any trouble with the comfort we ourselves receive from God. (2 Cor. 1:3–5)

Those are just a few of the many Bible verses confirming that we will have trouble in this life. But maybe you noticed that most of the verses also contain a *promise* from God for when we're in trouble. In nearly every case, we read that God will be our refuge and stronghold. He will keep us safe, hide us, set us on a rock. He will protect us, deliver us, and comfort us.

As for happiness in the life of Christians, take a look at these verses:

- May the righteous be glad and rejoice before God; may they be happy and joyful. (Ps. 68:3)
- Praise the LORD! Happy are those who fear the LORD. (Ps. 112:1 NRSV)
- Happy are the people whose God is the LORD! (Ps. 144:15 NKJV)
- To the person who pleases him, God gives wisdom, knowledge and happiness. (Eccl. 2:26)
- I know that there is nothing better for people than to be happy and to do good while they live. (Eccl. 3:12)

Other verses tell us always to be joyful, courageous, brave, confident, thankful — all sorts of positive things. God's will is, in fact, for his people to be happy — happy when things go right and also when things don't go right. Happiness, from God's point of view, shouldn't be dependent on our outward circumstances.

On what then, should we depend for our happiness?

True happiness, for the Christian, comes from our love relationship with our heavenly Father. That relationship trumps all else: a sordid past, a troubling present, and an unpredictable future. Of course, experiencing the happiness God intends for us depends on our willingness to trust him. We show trust by believing his Word and specifically his promises in the Bible. That's called *faith*. Faith in our God is a dominant theme throughout the Bible. We're told, in fact, that faith pleases God.

But can we really find happiness simply through having faith in God's promises? Is it possible to live worry-free when our marriage may be in jeopardy, our children are rebellious, our health is doubtful, our bank account is empty, and the news headlines cause us to shudder?

Yes, it is possible—no matter what. Trouble comes to us in all sorts of packages. Yours may be different from mine, and mine may be different from my neighbor's. But the remedy is still the same: *trusting in the power of God's promises as revealed to us in the Bible.*

Sometimes it seems like God sees to it that we have plenty of opportunities to put his promises to use. Those opportunities usually go by names like trouble, worry, illness, financial loss, broken relationships, and more. When we have such deep needs in our lives, if we listen closely, we can hear God calling, "Come closer, come closer."

One of the roughest times in my life came in the form of an economic disaster. I became very discouraged when there seemed to be no way out of my insurmountable problem. But then, at my lowest, God helped me see my situation from his point of view. I saw myself as caught in a raging river trying to swim upstream and getting nowhere fast. Then it was as if God said, "Let go, Nick. You can't swim against these waters. But if you'll let go and allow the rushing waters to pull you along, I promise you'll wash up on the shore of my will."

And so that's what I did. Over the course of the next several months, my situation didn't go away. In some ways, it got harder. And yet I had a peace that somehow it would all happen just as God promised—I would come out all right. Even better, I would come out on the sandy beach downstream—exactly where God wanted me to be.

It was at least two or three years later before I could finally say that horrible episode was behind me and I had indeed washed up on the shores of the perfect place God wanted me. Would I care to go through that experience again? No! But what I have now, I wouldn't trade for anything. *God came through.* His promise held firm.

How about you? Are you fighting against some raging waters right now? Are you facing something or someone that seems insurmountable? Or are you sailing along smoothly but hoping for a more fulfilling life? Either way, I hope you won't think I'm being simplistic when I tell you that God is for you. Grab hold of his promises, and don't let go. Trust him. Trust him. *Trust him.*

I'm not suggesting that you can simply use God's promises to pray away the trials in your life. That certainly didn't happen to me. Believing God's promises isn't an escape from reality or the troubles that plague us. But God's promises are stepping-stones for us to move on in life. The great English preacher Charles Spurgeon said that very thing: "The Bible is a book of precious promises; all the way we have to travel, they seem to be like a series of stepping-stones across the stream of time, and we may march from one promise to another, and never wet our feet all the way from earth to heaven, if we do but know how to keep our eyes open, and to find the right promise to step upon."

Power in the Promises is designed to help you keep your eyes open and find the right promises to step on as you journey from earth to heaven. My goal is to encourage you to trust God for great things in your life. If you're walking through a dense jungle right now, I want you to keep trudging straight ahead with the promises of God as your machete. The jungle will end. Stay the course. Hang tough with God. Use the promises and come out on the other side of this experience with more confidence in God than you have now. Whatever you do, don't get discouraged. Don't throw in the towel. *You will get through this.*

Despite all you're facing right now, all you've faced in the past (and the baggage you may still carry as a result), and all you'll face in the future, if you're a Christian, you have a source of happiness that trumps every obstacle you face.

And if you're one of those whose life is smooth sailing right now, then make use of the wind at your back. Raise the sails that are the promises of God's Word and see where he takes you.

So, are you ready to tap that source of happiness? Are you willing to be transformed over the course of the next several days, weeks, months, and years? The good news is that we can start our transformation now and be one day farther along tomorrow in our journey to a happy, productive life. That is what you want, isn't it? Happiness, closeness to God, usefulness, a sense of security that can't be shaken? I think that's what we all want.

The secret to that kind of life is a lot closer than you think. In fact, your life will begin to transform this very week as you put the principles in this book into practice.

Here's a verse about God's promises to help you get started. It tells us one reason God gives us his promises: "[God's] divine power has given us everything we need for a godly life through our knowledge of him who called us by his own glory and goodness. Through these he has given us *his very great and precious promises, so that through them you may participate in the divine nature, having escaped the corruption in the world caused by evil desires*" (2 Peter 1:3–4, italics mine). Did you catch that last part? Peter tells us the reason God has given us so many "great and precious promises" is that through them we might "participate in the divine nature" and escape "the corruption in the world caused by evil desires."

Sign me up!

Yes, the Bible is a book of promises given to every child of God so that he or she can overcome in every circumstance of life. The promises of God, when taken by faith, will absolutely transform us!

Christianity 101

This isn't some new teaching, it's been there all along. Down through the centuries, these same promises have transformed millions of believers just as they will transform anyone today who will dare to *believe* them, *say* them, and *pray* them. In past generations, this was Christianity 101.

Wisely did the nineteenth-century Scottish pastor and writer Andrew Bonar write, "Is Christ yours? Then his promises are yours."

Another great man of God from that century, D. L. Moody, wrote, "Thank God, none of those promises are out of date, or grown stale. They are as fresh and vigorous and young and sweet as ever." The problem is that many of us today seem to have forgotten how fresh God's promises are. Why is that?

Beth Moore asks us this very thing in her book *Believing God*. She writes, "God has made us promises. Real ones. Numerous ones. Promises of things like all-surpassing power, productivity, peace, and joy while still occupying these jars of clay. Few of us will argue the theory, but why aren't more of us living the reality?"[1] Perhaps we've grown so accustomed to modern life with all its shortcuts to our needs and "happiness" that unless we run into a crisis, we don't consider the importance of God's promises.

Men and women of old were often driven to God's promises by sheer necessity. Charles Spurgeon was a master at digging out the promises of God and standing on them, even as he suffered for many years from severe depression. In spite of that, he could write: "It is marvelous, brethren, how one sweet word of God will make whole songs for Christians. One word of God is like a piece of gold, and the Christian is the gold-beater, and he can hammer that promise out for whole weeks. I can say myself, I have lived on one promise for weeks, and want no other. I want just simply to hammer that promise out into gold-leaf, and plate my whole existence with joy from it."

The truth is that every Christian is richer than we realize — not monetarily, but in something even more important: rich in the "precious promises" that are rightfully ours.

---

1 Beth Moore, *Believing God* (Nashville: B&H, 2004), 4.

Another great hero of the faith who experienced the promises of God firsthand was George Mueller. As a young man, Mueller felt called of God to start an orphanage. And for the next fifty years of his life, the promises of God sustained his work with the thousands of children who passed through his homes. One of the promises he claimed early on was Psalm 81:10, "Open thy mouth wide, and I will fill it"(KJV). Mueller took this to mean that God was promising to supply all he would need in his ministry to the orphans. And God did. Years later, Mueller would remark, "If the Lord fails me at this time, it will be the first time." God did not fail Mueller — ever. Nor does he fail us.

Hudson Taylor was another one who lived on God's promises — and through him came the great China Inland Mission that has reached thousands of Chinese men and women for Christ. At one point in his ministry when he might have become discouraged, Taylor wrote to his wife, "We have twenty-five cents — and all the promises of God!" It was, of course, more than enough. The fruit from Hudson Taylor's work in China remains to this day.

In more recent times, we've seen examples of God fulfilling his promises in the lives of people like David Wilkerson, founder of Teen Challenge, a ministry to drug addicts and gang members he began in New York City. David started believing the promises of God as a teenager. In his classic book *The Cross and the Switchblade*, he tells of the time when he was the new student in school and had to face a bully. Not being a fighter, he turned to the Bible and claimed the promise in Zechariah 4:6: "Not by might, nor by power, but by my Spirit."

> When the time came to face Chuck, I decided I would simply lean on this promise. God would give me a holy boldness that would be equal to any bully.... Suddenly ahead I saw a boy walking toward me. I knew in an instant this would be Chuck. He was strutting down the opposite side of the street. But the instant he saw me, he crossed over and bore down on me like a heavy,

snorting angry bull. Chuck was an enormous boy. He must have weighed fifty pounds more than me, and he towered above me so that I had to bend my neck to look him in the eye. Chuck stopped dead in my path, legs spread and hands on his hips.

"You're the preacher's kid."

It wasn't a question; it was a challenge; and I'll admit that in that moment all my hopes of holy boldness vanished. I was scared to the core of me.

Not by might, nor by power, but by my Spirit. Not by might, nor by power, but by my Spirit saith the Lord of hosts. I kept repeating this sentence over and over to myself while Chuck commenced to give his opinion of me. First, he picked on the fact that I looked stupid in my new clothes. Then he worked over the obvious truth that I was a weakling. After that, he had a few words to say about preachers' kids in general.

By my Spirit saith the Lord. I still had not spoken, but inside me an amazing event was taking place. I felt fear melting, and in its place came confidence and joy. I looked up at Chuck and smiled.

Chuck was getting madder and madder. His face turned red as he challenged me to fight.

Still I smiled.

Chuck started to circle me with his fists clenched, pumping his arms slowly and taking short feints toward me. In his face though was a hint of alarm. He could see that, for some unfathomable reason, this little shrimp was truly not afraid.

I circled too, never taking my eyes off his, and all the while I smiled.

Finally Chuck hit me. It was a hesitant little blow that didn't hurt, and it happened to catch me on balance so I wasn't thrown. I laughed low and secretly.

Chuck stopped his circling. He dropped his fists. He backed off, and then he turned and took off down the street.

Next day at school I began to hear how I'd beaten up the biggest bully in town. Chuck had been telling everyone. He said I was the toughest guy he ever fought. Apparently he laid it on thick, because always after that I was treated with respect by the entire school. Perhaps I should have told the kids the truth, but I never did. I had a kind of insurance policy in my reputation. And hating to fight as I did, I wasn't about to turn my policy in.[2]

Many years later, a much older David Wilkerson could report, "As I look back over fifty years of ministry, I recall innumerable tests, trials, and times of crushing pain. But through it all, the Lord has proven faithful, loving, and totally true to all his promises."[3]

Not many of us are called to start ministries to drug addicts and gangs, but we each have tests, trials, and even crushing pains that come our way. And the promises of God will overcome every obstacle. Like David Wilkerson, we all have a God-designed destiny that we will only see happen as we lean hard on the promises of God for a lifetime.

Another more recent example of God fulfilling his promises can be seen in the life of Joni Eareckson Tada. Her trials came in the form of quadriplegia after a diving accident. Through her several decades in a wheelchair, Joni now says that for her, "real satisfaction comes not in understanding God's motives, but in understanding his character, in trusting in his promises, and in leaning on him and resting in him as the Sovereign who knows what he is doing and does all things well."[4]

Have you discovered that God does all things well? If you're a Christian who has been living below the spiritual poverty line for far too long, isn't it time to change that? Isn't it time to have the abundant life Jesus promised? To experience him doing "all things well" in your own life?

Good. Now let's take a look at what it means to go through life with the promises of God as our anchor.

---

2 David Wilkerson, *The Cross and the Switchblade* (Columbus, GA: Global Teen Challenge) 52–54. Used by permission.
3 David Wilkerson newsletter, June 13, 2005.
4 "Is God Really in Control?" *Joni and Friends*, 1987, 9.

The First Step: Believing the Promises of God

The first response God ever requires from a person is faith. It's through faith that we receive anything from God, including that very first step in the Christian life: believing in Christ and being born again as we receive him into our lives *by faith*. Some Christians mistakenly believe, however, that once we come to Christ by faith, the rest of the Christian life is simply going about the duties of a Christian: going to church, reading the Bible, praying hard, and staying away from evil.

But when Paul wrote to the Galatian believers who were trying to live out the Christian life by resorting to the law (doing the right things), he asked them, "Are you so foolish? After beginning by means of the Spirit, are you now trying to finish by means of the flesh? Have you experienced so much in vain—if it really was in vain? So again I ask, does God give you his Spirit and work miracles among you by the works of the law, or by your *believing what you heard*" (Gal. 3:3–5, italics mine).

The Christian life from start to finish is a life of believing what we have heard. And what we have heard is what is written to us in the Bible. We *hear* the Word. We *believe* the Word. We *pray* the Word. We *live* the Word. The promises of God are dead on the page unless we believe them and personally appropriate them for our own lives.

What do I mean by "appropriating" them? Well, let me use an old illustration of faith I learned when I first became a Christian. Let's say I walk up to you and hold out a present and say, "Here's a gift I bought for you. It's yours!" If your reaction is to say, "Gee, thanks," and you stand there looking at the gift in my hands but don't personally reach out and take it, it will not really be yours. It won't be yours even if you say, "I believe what you say. That present is mine. Thank you." The only way the gift becomes yours is when you "appropriate" it for yourself by reaching out and taking it in your own hands.

A similar illustration is to imagine walking up to me standing beside an empty chair. I say to you, "Here, have a seat." You reply, "Are you sure that chair will hold me? What if it falls apart the minute I sit in it?" I'd reply, "Oh, I'm sure it will hold you. It's a very finely made chair. No worries. Just sit." Even though you might then nod and believe me, when does your faith in my promise that the chair will hold you become real? Of course, it's when you actually place your weight fully in the chair by sitting in it. So it is with God's promises. It's not enough to say we believe; we must appropriate the promises by faith.

The Second Step: Saying What We Believe through Self-Talk

Believing in God's Word is the first step. But then declaring (mostly to our own ears) what we believe is a great way to renew our minds about the truth we profess to believe. To appropriate the promises of God in this book, *say them*.

What does it mean to "self-talk" what we believe? It simply means telling yourself the truth or stating one of God's promises about a given situation. Let's consider some common examples of how we already say the truth of God's Word. For many of us, it starts when we're young. Think back. Do you remember being taught prayers and creeds as a small child? I sure do. One of the creeds, or statements of faith, my parents taught me was the Apostles' Creed, which begins:

> I believe in God the Father Almighty,
> Maker of heaven and earth;
> And in Jesus Christ, his only Son, our Lord:
> who was conceived by the Holy Spirit,
> born of the Virgin Mary,
> suffered under Pontius Pilate,
> was crucified, dead, and buried....

Interestingly, the Apostles' Creed has been around since about the fourth century and is still used by several major Christian denominations. In that creed, Christians *say* exactly what we believe, and it works as a reminder of the truth.

In addition to learning prayers and creeds as a child, I (like you, no doubt) learned the great hymns of the faith through repetition. Every Sunday would find our congregation singing familiar stanzas from popular hymns such as "Blessed Assurance," "Rock of Ages," or "Amazing Grace." Just last Sunday, the church I now attend sang "Amazing Grace" again, and I was particularly struck by this verse, my favorite:

> The Lord has promis'd good to me,
> His word my hope secures;
> He will my shield and portion be
> As long as life endures.

I especially love the line that tells me God has promised "good" to me and that his Word, the Bible, my hope secures. When I sing those lines, it's a firm reminder of that vital truth.

Perhaps the granddaddy of the hymns about the promises of God is that oldie "Standing on the Promises." Take a listen to the words in these two stanzas:

> Standing on the promises that cannot fail!
> When the howling storms of doubt and fear assail,
> By the living Word of God I shall prevail,
> Standing on the promises of God.

> Standing on the promises of Christ the Lord,
> Bound to Him eternally by love's strong cord,
> Overcoming daily with the Spirit's Sword,
> Standing on the promises of God.

I love that imagery. "When the howling storms of doubt and fear assail, by the living Word of God I shall prevail" and "Bound to Him eternally by love's strong cord, overcoming daily with the

Spirit's Sword." Those words are as relevant to us today as they were when R. Kelso Carter wrote them in 1886.

Hymns, contemporary worship choruses, prayers, creeds, and even the childlike "Jesus Loves Me, This I Know" all serve as great reinforcers of what God has promised us in the Bible as we say or sing them. I know I need such ongoing reinforcement, and I bet you do too. During any given day, we all engage in some sort of self-talk. But too often our self-talk is along the lines of "I'm unhappy," "I can't do this," "I hate my life," "My marriage is shaky," "My kids are driving me crazy," "I failed again," "I'm not a very good Christian," or some other collection of accusations, discouraging words, or basic fault-finding with ourselves or others.

Sometimes though, we do get it right. Sometimes we do actually turn to the Bible for our internal self-talk. For instance, most Christians who have been faced with a challenge may have quoted to themselves, "I can do all things through Christ who strengthens me." That much-loved verse is, of course, from Philippians 4:13 (NKJV). Surely when Paul wrote those words it was an encouragement to the hearers of his letter in Philippi, but it was also no doubt something Paul deeply believed for himself.

Other biblical characters also engaged in self-talk. David was the number one self-talker in the Bible. Many of his psalms are vigorous self-talk. David even admits this when he speaks directly to his soul, commanding it to "bless the Lord." Listen as David talks to his soul in the opening verses of Psalm 103:

> Bless the LORD, O my soul;
> And all that is within me, bless His holy name!
> Bless the LORD, O my soul,
> And forget not all His benefits:
> Who forgives all your iniquities,
> Who heals all your diseases,
> Who redeems your life from destruction,
> Who crowns you with lovingkindness and tender mercies,

Who satisfies your mouth with good things,
So that your youth is renewed like the eagle's. (vv. 1 – 5 NKJV)

Now, *that's* the kind of self-talk we all need once in a while.

Probably the most well-known section of scriptural self-talk is David's Twenty-Third Psalm. In the first four verses, David affirms his faith through self-talk. Then, at the end of verse 4 and into verse 5, he turns his self-talk into prayer — *praying the promises* — before concluding with the affirmation that goodness and mercy shall follow him all his days and he will dwell in the house of the Lord forever.

> The LORD is my shepherd;
> I shall not want.
> He makes me to lie down in green pastures;
> He leads me beside the still waters.
> He restores my soul;
> He leads me in the paths of righteousness
> For His name's sake.
>
> Yea, though I walk through the valley of the shadow of death,
> I will fear no evil;
> For You are with me;
> Your rod and Your staff, they comfort me.
>
> You prepare a table before me in the presence of my enemies;
> You anoint my head with oil;
> My cup runs over.
> Surely goodness and mercy shall follow me
> All the days of my life;
> And I will dwell in the house of the LORD
> Forever. (NKJV)

Go back and read that psalm aloud to yourself. Mean what you say. This is God's Word to you. Go ahead, I'll wait.

✣ ✣ ✣

That was powerful, wasn't it?

Hannah Whitall Smith was a devout Christian woman who in 1875 wrote one of the bestselling books of all time. To date, it has sold millions of copies and is still widely read. I highly recommend it. The title? *The Christian's Secret of a Happy Life.* Hannah knew about self-talk and the promises of God. She tells how she learned to self-talk the Twenty-Third Psalm:

> The Twenty-Third Psalm had, of course, always been familiar to me from my nursery days, but it had never seemed to have any special meaning. Then came a critical moment in my life when I was sadly in need of comfort but could see none anywhere. I could not at the moment lay my hands on my Bible, and I cast about in my mind for some passage of Scripture that would help me. Immediately there flashed into my mind the words, "The Lord is my shepherd, I shall not want." At first I turned from it almost with scorn. "Such a common text as that," I said to myself, "is not likely to do me any good"; and I tried hard to think of a more [relevant] one, but none would come; and at last it almost seemed as if there were no other text in the whole Bible. And finally I was reduced to saying, "Well, if I cannot think of any other text, I must try to get what little good I can out of this one," and I began to repeat to myself over and over, "The Lord is my shepherd, I shall not want." Suddenly, as I did so, the words were divinely illuminated, and there poured out upon me such floods of comfort that I felt as if I could never have a trouble again.
>
> The moment I could get hold of a Bible, I turned over its leaves with eagerness to see whether it could possibly be true that such untold treasures of comfort were really and actually mine, and whether I might dare to let out my heart into the full enjoyment of them. And I did what I have often found great profit in doing: I built up a pyramid of declarations and promises concerning the Lord being our Shepherd that, once built, presented an immovable and indestructible front to all

the winds and storms of doubt or trial that could assail it. And I became convinced, beyond a shadow of doubt, that the Lord really was my Shepherd, and that in giving himself this name he assumed the duties belonging to the name, and really would be, what he declares himself to be, a "good shepherd who giveth his life for his sheep."

The Twenty-Third Psalm has been a lifesaver for many, as have various other of David's psalms. But David wasn't the only person in the Bible to engage in self-talk. We read in Lamentations that the prophet Jeremiah knew the value of self-talk. He wrote:

> Because of the LORD's great love we are not consumed,
>> for his compassions never fail.
> They are new every morning;
>> great is your faithfulness.
> *I say to myself*, "The LORD is my portion;
>> therefore I will wait for him."
>
> The LORD is good to those whose hope is in him,
>> to the one who seeks him;
> it is good to wait quietly
>> for the salvation of the LORD. (Lam. 3:22–26, italics mine)

That's self-talk of the highest order. Finding a promise ("The LORD is my portion") and coming to a conclusion about one's situation ("therefore I will wait for him") based on that promise is life-changing!

Another well-known Old Testament verse that urges biblical self-talk is Joel 3:10, which urges, "Let the weak say, 'I am strong'" (NKJV). That's a thought we find echoed in the New Testament when Paul writes, "For when I am weak, then I am strong" (2 Cor. 12:10). That's another verse many Christians routinely say to themselves during a trial. It's also one that's often prayed by Christians as we turn to God and confess, "Lord, I'm weak! But in you I know I'm strong! I can handle this with your strength!"

Another New Testament example of self-talk is found in Hebrews 13:5 – 6 (italics mine):

Keep your lives free from the love of money and be content with what you have, because God has said,

"Never will I leave you;
  never will I forsake you."

So we say with confidence,

"The Lord is my helper; I will not be afraid.
  What can mere mortals do to me?"

Just as there have been many great Christians of the past who *believed* God's promises, so too were there those who *spoke* God's truth to themselves through their own confessions or resolutions based on God's Word. Two good examples are Puritan writer Thomas Brooks and the great American theologian Jonathan Edwards. Here's what Brooks confessed to himself regularly:

I am his by purchase and I am his by conquest.
I am his by donation and I am his by election;
I am his by covenant and I am his by marriage;
I am wholly his; I am particularly his;
I am universally his; I am eternally his.

Thomas, that's good preaching to yourself! I'm sure he blessed his own soul every time he offered up those words, which are all based on promises God has given us in the Bible. A person who grasps those lines and *owns* them cannot be an unhappy person.

As for Jonathan Edwards, he extracted truth from the Bible and applied it to his life in the form of "resolutions."

At barely age twenty, Edwards wrote out what he called his "resolutions." Although there are a total of seventy resolutions (half of which were written in just two sittings), I'll list just a few, realizing that what was a resolution for Edwards may not be a resolution for you or me. Self-talk is like that. What I may need to say in the way of self-talk may be entirely different on some points than what you must say to yourself.

Edwards's practice was to read his seventy resolutions once a week, and he did so for the next thirty-five years. At the time of his death in 1758, he had read through his resolutions more than eighteen hundred times. Now, that's reinforcement. That's transformation.

Apparently Edwards, like us, was only too aware of his own lack of strength in keeping his resolutions, thus he prefaced them by saying, "Being sensible that I am unable to do anything without God's help, I do humbly entreat him, by his grace, to enable me to keep these Resolutions, so far as they are agreeable to his will, for Christ's sake."

Here are just a few of his seventy "self-talk" resolutions, all based on a firm belief in the Bible's promises as his foundation:

- *Resolved*, To live with all my might, while I do live.
- *Resolved*, Never to do any thing, which I should be afraid to do if it were the last hour of my life.
- *Resolved*, Never to do any thing out of revenge.
- *Resolved*, To study the Scriptures so steadily, constantly, and frequently, as that I may find, and plainly perceive, myself to grow in the knowledge of the same.
- I frequently hear persons in old age say how they would live, if they were to live their lives over again: *Resolved*, That I will live just so as I can think I shall wish I had done, supposing I live to old age.

The Third Step: Praying the Promises

Having believed God's promise and having "self-talked" it, the next thing we can do is *pray* God's promise. As the great Bible commentator Matthew Henry said, "God's promises are to be our pleas in prayer." For instance, in the example I used from Lamentations, can you imagine how Jeremiah might have prayed? I'm sure it was along the lines of "Lord, you are my portion, therefore I will wait for you. You, O Lord, are good to those who hope in you, to those who seek you. It is good, Lord, to wait quietly for your salvation."

But biblical self-talk and praying God's promises were not just for David or Paul or even the likes of Matthew Henry, Hannah Whitall Smith, Thomas Brooks, Jonathan Edwards, and David Wilkerson. *Any* Christian can be — and should be — transformed by living on God's promises.

Part 2 of *Power in the Promises* is all about applying God's Word in your unique situations and trials. It's about ceasing to think (and react) like men and women who don't have a trustworthy God and beginning to act like those who have a heavenly Father who watches over our every circumstance. It's about leaving our spiritual poverty behind and taking up the treasures of God's Word. It's about developing the practice of looking to the Bible and extracting promises that were meant for us and then speaking and praying them into our lives. It's about changing how we think by renewing our mind with God's Word. After all, Paul instructs us in Romans 12:2 to "be transformed by the renewing of your mind."

I've found that speaking God's Word to myself or to God through prayer *does* transform me. The more I intake God's Word, the more my mind changes from the negative, self-absorbed me to the confident, happy me that's looking to fulfill God's destiny for me. The same will be true for you.

But *are* there Bible promises that speak to our every circumstance? Yes, there are. Many of them you'll find on the following pages. Others you will discover for yourself. Some promises may not be stated as such, but because the Bible is a book of truth, inherent in each truth is a promise to be believed.

What are the results of living by God's promises? How about overcoming obstacles in your life? How about enjoying a deeper relationship with God? Or how about reaping a glorious destiny? God has designed each of us uniquely, and his promises will be fulfilled in your life by faith, in accordance with his faithfulness and his desired end for you.

I want to share an example of someone who has overcome great hardship through the power of God's promises. Not long ago, I met a woman named Faye Byrd at a conference. When I told her about the book I was writing on the promises of God, she told me her story, and when I returned home, she sent me a copy of the short book she had written about her recovery from a traumatic brain injury after years of frustration, despair, and utter hopelessness. The following is an excerpt from her book *Hope Restored*:

> Thinking in my heart and believing what God's Word said about me, for his Word is truth, set me free. The washing of the water of the Word washed my mind and planted hope in my mind and soul. Where it grew, it produced leaves, flowers, and the fruit of wellness in my mind, watering my mind, which still flows today. I had been thinking of the injury and disability as a deformity. This was not the truth. Through God's Word, I learned and started to believe that:
>
> > I was a winner and not a loser.
> > I had the mind of Christ.
> > God loved and accepted me unconditionally.
> > He created me because he wanted me.
>
> In addition, I was not accepted based on my abilities and performances, but through Jesus, I am one of the beloved. So accepting the truth that I am fearfully and wonderfully made as a child of God, I started to walk in the truth of who I am in Christ Jesus.
> I had been a born-again believer since I was twenty-six years of age, but due to the memory loss following the head trauma, I was learning anew what God's Word says about me. This

relearning of who I am in Christ led to contentment.... God took my fragmented and broken life, integrating it and putting it together. He did what all the medical personnel, technology, and medicine could not do, making me into something beautiful. No longer was I Humpty Dumpty, broken. I was standing on the solid rock, chipped, but not destroyed.

The reforming of the vessel of my life is in the hands of the potter, God, and he is forming this new personality into the vessel he desires. I have been broken and spilled, but I was not wasted. All things are possible for God. He restored hope in my heart through his Word. And there was light at the end of the tunnel.[5]

Faye mentioned hope—and faith in God's promises generates hope. That hope is made real as we pray God's promises and believe that "He who promised is faithful" (Heb. 10:23).

The late Dr. Robert Cook, author of the classic book for new Christians *Now That I Believe*, told of the time he arrived in Korea at four in the morning for a prayer meeting scheduled that day. To his surprise, the church was already packed with thousands of people, many of them pouring over their Bibles. He approached one dear woman and asked why so many had already gathered at such an early hour. She replied, "We're here early so we can look up promises that we can throw up to heaven when we pray."

Are you ready to "throw promises up to heaven" when you pray? Are you ready to discover the power in God's promises for yourself? Good!

The format of the rest of *Power in the Promises* is simple. Each entry deals with a particular life issue many of us face. First, I present one or more scriptural promises that address the issue ("The Truth according to God's Word"). Then I offer a brief paragraph ("The Truth") that describes the situation. This is followed by a suggested affirmation, or self-talk ("Tell Yourself the

---

5 Faye Nunnelee Byrd, *Hope Restored: The Fork in the Road, Following a Traumatic Brain Injury* (Bloomington, IN: WestBow, 2013), 22–23.

Truth"), to help you begin thinking about your life through the lens of God's Word. Then I offer a suggested prayer ("Pray the Promise") that puts the words of the promise into a plea to God to work the transformation as you believe and speak the promises into your life. Occasionally, as a reinforcement of sorts, I include a sidebar quote from one of my favorite Christian authors to add a final touch to that particular topic.

As you read the self-talk and pray the promise in a particular selection, make what you read your own. Don't just read words off the page. Instruct your soul — as did David — in the words of Scripture.

A Few Final Cautions

Now, before you dig in, here are a few words of advice:

- The first promise of God any of us needs to appropriate is the promise of eternal life. All of God's promises are for his children. Becoming his child happens as a result of believing God's promise about eternal life and salvation — about believing Christ died for you. So if this is all new to you, I'd like you to turn to page 249 ("I Believe in the Lord Jesus Christ. Salvation is Fully Mine") and accept God's invitation to become his child. When you do, a whole new world opens for you. And that world includes his many promises for his children.

- Reading and praying the Scriptures needs to be more than a one-time experience, because renewing the mind takes time. You'll need to make it a lifelong habit to rely on the promises of the Bible to take you through the highs and lows of life. But if you will begin today to saturate yourself with the promises of God, you will also begin today to see your transformation. Remember, for years you've been repeating the same defeating self-talk, so your transformation will take time — but perhaps not as long as you think. My guess is that within a week you'll notice a difference in your outlook. Just be willing to start where you are, not where you wish you were. This is a long-term project, but the results are well worth the journey.

- God's Word is full of promises for every believer, but those promises must not be mishandled. Never try to use Scripture to "confess" or self-talk your way into having something that clearly isn't God's will. In short, don't use Scripture to justify selfish needs or desires. Prayerfully seek God's will for your life, and then allow the Word to guide you in the pursuit of the destiny God has for you. Believing, saying, and praying is not some magic formula. Saying the words, even believing them, as important as that is, is really only the gateway to where you want to go. The purpose of believing, saying, and praying God's promises is that you'll then be able to *live* the promises. If you don't live them, this all becomes just a mental exercise, and that's not what God wants for you.

- Don't just read the "Tell Yourself the Truth" sections in your head. Speak them aloud when you can. Your goal is to internalize them. Speaking them out loud, when practical, can help you do that. Same with the "Pray the Truth" sections. If at all possible, pray aloud in private.

- For the purposes of this book, I'm only able to include a limited number of promises and the issues they address. Mostly I've chosen common issues many of us face. But you may have unique situations in your life that aren't covered here. I hope that as you read this book, you'll begin to identify your areas of weakness and find appropriate verses that will help you lay claim to the promises that will help you. Some such topics might include suicidal temptations, bipolar issues, broken marriages, or specific relational problems. Or you might need specific promises because you are in the military or are a prisoner, a teenager, or a missionary. For each of these, you can find a way to "tell yourself the truth" about your situation—and it will change your life for the better. On page 314 I conclude the book with two exercises to get you started on additional topics relevant to problems unique to you.

- Remember, sometimes a promise isn't overtly stated but is inherent in the truth of the passage. If a verse isn't a "promise" per se, look to its truth and extract the promise consistent with that truth.

- As you read through the topics on the following pages, turn to the Bible and discover additional verses on those topics you can own as God's truth. When you see a verse that speaks to your need, write the Scripture down, and then write out a declaration or affirmation of how that verse applies to *you*. Make it as personal as possible. There are *many* verses on the topics in this book that I simply didn't have room to include. Search them out!

- When you find circumstances in your life that tempt you to pull away from the Word as your compass, I want you to think about Rick, a friend of mine from church. Rick tells me that when he was a boy, his father took him out hunting for the first time and gave him a compass. He told Rick, "Son, when you're lost and you look at your compass and think it must be wrong, that's the time you need to trust it." So it is with the Bible. When you're most tempted to doubt it, that's when to adhere to its truth.

- Don't forget that the promises are meant to draw us closer to the Promiser. When the promise becomes more important than fellowship with God, you've gone into error. Don't do that. Remember these words from Hannah Whitall Smith: "It is grand to trust in the promises, but it is grander still to trust in the Promiser."

- Keep in mind that appropriating the promises of God is just one of several important aspects of the Christian life. Walking in the Holy Spirit, being part of a vital Christian fellow-ship, and experiencing intimacy with Christ are also keys to transformation. In previous books, I've written about the importance of both prayer (*Magnificent Prayer*) and Christ indwelling the Christian (*His Victorious Indwelling*). Don't focus on one element of the Christian life to the exclusion of other components. They all work together to transform us into vital Christians with a destiny to live out for God.

• Heed this warning from D. L. Moody about harboring sin in your life: "If we are regarding iniquity in our hearts, or living on a mere empty profession, we have no claim to expect that our prayers will be answered. There is not one solitary promise for us. I sometimes tremble when I hear people quote promises, and say that God is bound to fulfill those promises to them, when all the time there is something in their own lives which they are not willing to give up. It is well for us to search our hearts and find out why it is that our prayers are not answered." My assumption, however, is that if you're reading this, you are a growing Christian, desiring to please the Lord.

I would be remiss not to point out that the promises in the Bible fall into two categories: unconditional promises and conditional promises. Unconditional promises are promises God makes that will be fulfilled regardless of what we do. Such promises include God's promise never again to destroy the world through a flood (Gen. 9:8–11), Christ's promise to return for his own (John 14:3 et al.), and God's promise never to leave us or forsake us (Heb. 13:5).

Conditional promises are usually easily evident by the words around them. Consider these verses and identify the condition:

• "If you remain in me and my words remain in you, ask whatever you wish, and it will be done for you." (John 15:7)
• If any of you lacks wisdom, you should ask God, who gives generously to all without finding fault, and it will be given

to you. But when you ask, you must believe and not doubt, because the one who doubts is like a wave of the sea, blown and tossed by the wind. That person should not expect to receive anything from the Lord. (James 1:5–7)

- Submit yourselves, then, to God. Resist the devil, and he will flee from you. Come near to God and he will come near to you. (James 4:7–8)

- "If my people, who are called by my name, will humble themselves and pray and seek my face and turn from their wicked ways, then I will hear from heaven, and I will forgive their sin and will heal their land." (2 Chron. 7:14)

Don't let God's conditional promises make you reluctant to claim them. His conditions are not hard to fulfill. Even John 3:16 ("For God so loved the world that he gave his one and only Son, that whoever believes in him shall not perish but have eternal life") is a conditional promise, but believing in him is something you can do. Faith is a condition for many of God's promises, and God will not ask you to exercise faith without giving you the ability to do so.

Now, as you dig into God's promises, remember, God wants you to expect more from him than you're presently experiencing. He wants to be your Provider, Comforter, Counselor, Protector— well, your Everything! He's bigger than you can possibly imagine and able to do "immeasurably more than all we ask or imagine, according to his power that is at work within us" (Eph. 3:20). His promises are his invitation to a happy life.

My prayer for you is that God will continually speak to you through the promises of the Bible. I pray that this book will launch you on your own expedition of searching out the promises in God's Word. Those promises are given just for you! Don't neglect them. *Live them!*

PART 2

SELF-TALK TOPICS

Put your will then over on to the believing side.
Say, "Lord I will believe, I do believe,"
and continue to say it. Insist upon believing,
in the face of every suggestion of doubt with which you
may be tempted. Out of your very unbelief,
throw yourself headlong onto the word and promises of God,
and dare to abandon yourself to the keeping and saving power
of the Lord Jesus. If you have ever trusted a precious interest
in the hands of any earthly friend, I entreat you,
trust yourself now and all your spiritual interests
in the hands of your Heavenly Friend,
and never, never, NEVER allow yourself
to doubt again.

HANNAH WHITALL SMITH

I **Abide** in Christ

The Truth according to God's Word

"Abide in Me, and I in you. As the branch cannot bear fruit of itself, unless it abides in the vine, neither can you, unless you abide in Me. I am the vine, you are the branches. He who abides in Me, and I in him, bears much fruit; for without Me you can do nothing." (John 15:4–5 NKJV)

The Truth

When we feel dissatisfied, not useful to God and others, what's the likely reason? Often it's related to our misunderstanding of our true source of spiritual life—Jesus. We're like branches that have been disconnected from the grapevine. Too often we forget our true source of life and turn back to the very things that can never satisfy, thus cutting ourselves off from him. Yet Jesus' promise still stands: "He who abides in Me, and I in him, bears much fruit." So too does the other promise in this verse: "Without Me you can do nothing."

Tell Yourself the Truth

"God has placed me in Christ. He is my Vine, and I am his branch. In him I abide and bear much fruit. Abiding apart from him, I bear no fruit; in fact, apart from him, I can do nothing. All that God has called me to do can be fully accomplished through abiding in Christ. My life is fruitful as his life flows through me, nourishing me. I am safe in Christ, fully attached to my True Vine."

Pray the Promise

Father, you have placed me in Christ. He is my Vine, and I'm but a branch. As I bear fruit, I know it's not fruit that comes from me on my own. Rather, any fruit from my life is a natural result of abiding in Christ. And that fruit, Lord, is good fruit. I pray you bear more fruit—much more fruit through me as I make Christ my True Vine and home.

∽

"Abide in me," says Jesus. "Cling to me. Stick fast to me. Live the life of close and intimate communion with me. Get nearer to me. Roll every burden on me. Cast your whole weight on me. Never let go your hold on me for a moment. Be, as it were, rooted and planted in me. Do this and I will never fail you. I will ever abide in you."

—J. C. RYLE

God Is the Source of My Abundant Supply

The Truth according to God's Word

Those who seek the LORD lack no good thing. (Ps. 34:10)

For the LORD God is a sun and shield;
    the LORD bestows favor and honor;
no good thing does he withhold
    from those whose walk is blameless. (Ps. 84:11)

And my God shall supply all your need according to His riches in glory by Christ Jesus. (Phil. 4:19 NKJV)

The Truth

In Christ, God desires to meet all our needs in abundance. His promise is that we shall lack no good thing and that he will meet our need according to his *riches* in Christ Jesus. We can rest assured that there is abundance for our needs in Christ. Often we make the mistake of defining our needs according to our own imaginations and expecting God to provide for them. What if, instead, we were to define our needs by looking at God's provision? We're often disappointed when we don't get as much as we think we need. But God has made no promise to give us our imaginary needs. Our abundance comes from being satisfied with the Provider, not looking at the provision.

Tell Yourself the Truth

"God is my great Provider. In him, I lack nothing. God supplies my every need according to his riches in glory, not according to my meager resources. Therefore I don't lean on any person for my supply, for people will eventually disappoint. With God's never-ending and never-disappointing provision, I am satisfied. I want for nothing. God gives me above and beyond what I need so that I can share with others. I suffer no lack now, nor will I in the future. His promise is good for eternity."

Pray the Promise

Father, you supply me with an abundance of good things — both spiritually and materially. All my blessings have their source in you. I lack nothing because my eyes are on you, not on my material goods. You anticipate my every need and will do so for the rest of my life and on into eternity. Thank you, Father, for the overflow of good things in my life.

∽

"The Bible is full of God's promises to provide for us spiritually and materially, to never forsake us, to give us peace in times of difficult circumstances, to cause all circumstances to work together for our good, and finally to bring us safely home to glory. Not one of those promises is dependent upon our performance. They are all dependent on the grace of God given to us through Jesus Christ."

— JERRY BRIDGES

In Christ, I Am Stronger Than My **Addictions**

The Truth according to God's Word

"If the Son sets you free, you will be free indeed." (John 8:36)

For we know that our old self was crucified with him so that the body ruled by sin might be done away with, that we should no longer be slaves to sin—because anyone who has died has been set free from sin. (Rom. 6:6–7)

If anyone is in Christ, he is a new creation; the old has gone, the new has come! (2 Cor. 5:17)

So I say, walk by the Spirit, and you will not gratify the desires of the flesh. (Gal. 5:16)

The Truth

Addictions are devastating. We lose our very identities to that which enslaves us, whether it be alcohol, drugs, sex, or anything else. *To be addicted is to be in chains.* But when Christ purchased us and made us his own, he made it possible for us to leave our other masters and become a slave to him only. We became new creations—the old is gone forever. When we live that promise by faith, it becomes our reality. The only good thing our addiction ever did was drive us to Christ in whom we find freedom. *Believe* for freedom. *Speak* freedom—and *keep* speaking it. Then pray it and live it. Don't ever turn back.

Tell Yourself the Truth

"I was once a slave to my addiction, but now, in Christ, that addiction is forever broken. The 'old man' who was entrapped by his fleshly addictions is dead and gone. I now live new life in Christ. Yes, my body still tries to tell me it needs 'just one more' walk down the road that leads to my ruin. But I have been purchased by Christ, and my body is not my own anymore. I no longer have to obey its cravings. When Christ took away my sins, he took possession of me entirely. I am owned by Christ, a slave to Christ—and to be a slave to Christ means to be set free from anything else that would enslave me. Christ will not share me with my old slave master. As I walk in the Spirit, I don't fulfill the addictive desires of my flesh. The power of God within me helps me draw boundaries to keep me away from going back to my addictions. I stay away from the people, places, and situations that lure me back to where I never want to go again. I'm much happier with the joy of Christ, which far outweighs the temporary high of my addiction. Christ now owns me, and I now own my freedom."

Pray the Promise

Thank you, God, for all the men and women down through the ages whom you have delivered from severe addictions. I count myself as one of those who has been set free in you. I praise you that when I'm tempted, I can turn to you and find a way of escape. I thank you that when I mess up, I find forgiveness in you. And I thank you that as time passes, the urgency of my addiction passes as your healing becomes more real to me than the strong desires of my flesh. That can only be you at work in my life. I stand tall and free, bold and unafraid because of my freedom. Praise you, Lord!

∽

"Habits have deep roots. Once sin is allowed to settle in your heart, it will not be turned out at your bidding. Custom becomes second nature, and its chains are not easily broken."

—J. C. RYLE

Adversity Only Makes Me Stronger

The Truth according to God's Word

The righteous person may have many troubles,
    but the LORD delivers him from them all. (Ps. 34:19)

If you faint in the day of adversity,
Your strength is small. (Prov. 24:10 NKJV)

The Truth

The presence of adversity doesn't mean the absence of God. In fact, God is ever present in our adversity. God never permits adversity that doesn't have a desired end from his point of view. *Don't waste your adversities.* Let every adversity bear its good fruit in due time.

Tell Yourself the Truth

"There is no adversity under the sun that can take me down. None! God sees and knows all that's happening to me, especially this present adversity—and he is here in his great strength. There is no way I will not come through this stronger than ever. This adversity has spiritual growth written all over it. While it presses into me, I press all the harder into Christ. The greater the adversity, the closer to Christ I come. Job knew adversity. Moses knew adversity. Naomi, Esther, David, Paul—and especially Jesus—all knew adversity. In every case, they came victoriously out of the tunnel of adversity in God's due time. *And so will I.*"

Pray the Promise

God, this adversity will not take me down. I have entrusted you with this agonizing situation and know you have it resolved even now; I only need to watch it play out in your hands and know that you work for my good. I will keep my eyes on you and not on the situation. You have made me a victor in all my adversities, and I praise you, Father.

~

"Adversity is not simply a tool. It is God's most effective tool for the advancement of our spiritual lives. The circumstances and events that we see as setbacks are oftentimes the very things that launch us into periods of intense spiritual growth. Once we begin to understand this, and accept it as a spiritual fact of life, adversity becomes easier to bear."

—CHARLES STANLEY

God Speaks to Me in My Afflictions

The Truth according to God's Word

"He speaks to them in their affliction." (Job 36:15)

I will be glad and rejoice in your love,
    for you saw my affliction
    and knew the anguish of my soul. (Ps. 31:7)

Be joyful in hope, patient in affliction, faithful in prayer. (Rom. 12:12)

The Truth

When we suffer affliction, God knows the anguish of our souls. *He knows!* We can rejoice—hard as it may be—and listen as God speaks to us. No, we don't like afflictions, but the truth is that they can make us or break us. Which will it be?

Tell Yourself the Truth

"God sees my affliction. He knows my anguish. He has heard my cries in the night. But during my affliction, my hope is securely in him as I wait patiently and pray my way through. I will not be overcome by this affliction. Yes, it tests my patience—but I shall pass the test, standing strong, rejoicing in God's love. I will emerge from this affliction stronger than I have ever been, and when it has passed, all the praise goes to God because he has been with me during the entire ordeal, making me stronger, more trusting, and a witness to what God can do through a surrendered trial or affliction."

Pray the Promise

Lord, you know how hard this is. And yet I have your promise that you speak to me through my affliction, that you know the anguish of my soul, and that you ask me only to be patient as I pray my way through this season. I will be glad and rejoice, knowing your eyes never glance away from me—not for a second. I will draw goodness from what seems to be such a hard time. I believe this trial will work to my good.

⤳

"When I am in the cellar of affliction, I look for the Lord's choicest wines."

— SAMUEL RUTHERFORD

Aging Can Be a Blessing, Not a Curse

The Truth according to God's Word

"My days are swifter than a runner; they fly away." (Job 9:25)

"Even to your old age and gray hairs
   I am he, I am he who will sustain you.
I have made you and I will carry you;
   I will sustain you and I will rescue you." (Isa. 46:4)

The Truth

Growing old is a gift from God. We are meant to enjoy, not resent, our later years. But sometimes illness, aches and pains, loss of finances, and loneliness all seem to work against what should be a joyous season of life. God knew we would need him in a different way as we age, and he is ready with his promises to keep us in the grip of his hand until the day we see him face-to-face. And each day we age brings us one day closer to spending eternity with our Father in the glory and promise of our new lives and new bodies.

Tell Yourself the Truth

"God has granted me the gift of years, and I'm grateful. There are valleys to be sure, but God dwells with those who are in the valley.

Others may waste their second half of life, but I will not. I will keep on going—persevering, interceding, rejoicing, serving until the day he calls me home. I look back through the years of my life and see how God has carried me this far. He will not desert me now. He will carry me, he will sustain me, he will rescue me as I age with grace. I have nothing to fear in growing older. This is God's Word to me."

Pray the Promise

Thank you, Lord, for this autumn season of my life. Though I desire to be with you in eternity, I'm happy to remain here as an intercessor and a witness for you and to continue to revel in your presence. Yes, in my final years, I will be a worshiper of you. I will rejoice in you. In hard times and good times, I will praise you, my Lord.

⌒

"I shall grow old, but never lose life's zest,
because the road's last turn will be the best."
—HENRY VAN DYKE

God Has Assigned Angels to Watch Over Me

The Truth according to God's Word

He will command his angels concerning you
to guard you in all your ways. (Ps. 91:11)

Are not all angels ministering spirits sent to serve those who will
inherit salvation? (Heb. 1:14)

The Truth

We are guarded at all times by an unseen realm of protecting
angels. They keep our every way. And they are experts at what
they do.

Tell Yourself the Truth

"I'm an inheritor of salvation, and God's ministering angels are
sent to guard me in all my ways. Though I don't see these protec-
tors, I know that God works through them to accomplish his will
for me and to see me kept safe. When I sense trouble on the way,
I smile, knowing God's angels are gathering nearby. I thank God
for his angels working on my behalf."

Pray the Promise

Father, it seems enough that you watch over me, but that you should dispatch angels to my care thrills me. Thank you for these unseen guardians. May I never be in such a rush that I run faster than my angels can fly.

～

"Believers, look up — take courage. The angels are nearer than you think."

— BILLY GRAHAM

I Am Slow to **Anger**, Always Forgiving

The Truth according to God's Word

Refrain from anger and turn from wrath;
  do not fret—it leads only to evil. (Ps. 37:8)

[Love] is not easily angered, it keeps no record of wrongs. (1 Cor. 13:5)

The Truth

Anger is a quick-moving emotion. Certain circumstances can set any of us off. Yet we know that God has called us to love, not unrighteous anger. How then can we avoid flying off the handle so easily? One way is by relinquishing control. Often our anger is stirred up when we feel a loss of control in a situation. But by giving up control and putting the outcome in God's hands, we can avoid anger. We can let out a deep breath of relief and exchange our pull toward anger with a pull toward a better emotion: *love*. When our anger is righteous anger—the kind of anger God also feels—we still must take our feelings to him and talk with him about the situation. God is a good listener when we need to vent, and he will help us respond as we should.

Tell Yourself the Truth

"In Christ, I am not an angry person. I'm called to love and peace, not to divisiveness and fighting. Anger only leads me to greater evil — and to sin. When I'm angry, I say things I don't mean and later regret my words and my actions, often hurting those I love. When I'm tempted to anger, I will pray for those who would anger me, realizing that God has forgiven me for many, many offenses and that I, in turn, can forgive those who wrong me. I release them from my anger, I release all bitterness, and invite love to replace feelings of revenge, malice, and unforgiveness. When my anger is directed at a situation, I stop and do nothing until I pray and wait. I ask God if this is a control issue — and he always answers."

Pray the Promise

God, I hate what happens when I become angry. I hate the repair work that must occur when I've wrongly blown off steam at some person or situation that ticked me off. Help me to make your ears the first that hear my complaints when I get angry. Calm me down by reassuring me that you know the end of the situation and that all will be well. I realize that my anger doesn't need to be part of the solution to any situation. Please give me your peace and self-control.

⌒

"Do not say, 'I cannot help having a bad temper.' Friend, you must help it. Pray to God to help you overcome it at once, for either you must kill it, or it will kill you. You cannot carry a bad temper into heaven."

— CHARLES SPURGEON

I Cast My **Anxiety** on God

The Truth according to God's Word

Search me, God, and know my heart;
   test me and know my anxious thoughts. (Ps. 139:23)

Do not be anxious about anything, but in every situation, by prayer and petition, with thanksgiving, present your requests to God. (Phil. 4:6)

The Truth

Anxiety is fear of the unknown. A major source of anxiety comes from not knowing what will happen next on the world stage or on the smaller pedestals of our lives. But we often forget that what is unknown to us is fully known to God. Rather than letting anxiety shape us, we can allow God's faithfulness to mold us. He can be trusted in every anxious situation—whether it's on the large stage of world events or, more likely, in the smaller anxieties that rob us of joy in our relationships, careers, and families.

Tell Yourself the Truth

"Anxiety robs me of peace and undermines my faith. I will therefore obey God's Word and not be anxious about anything. In every anxious situation, through prayer and thanksgiving, I will release my anxiety to God, exchanging it for his peace. He will still my every anxious thought."

Pray the Promise

Father, I release all anxiety to you. All sense of panic or unfounded nervousness must be replaced by my confidence in you. Your peace is my only antidote for needless anxiety. I will rest in you, the one who never has a cause for anxiety.

⌒

"I am no longer anxious about anything, as I realize the Lord is able to carry out his will, and his will is mine. It makes no matter where he places me, or how. That is rather for him to consider than for me; for in the easiest positions he must give me his grace, and in the most difficult, his grace is sufficient."

— HUDSON TAYLOR

The **Bible** Reveals God to Me

The Truth according to God's Word

We also thank God continually because, when you received the word of God, which you heard from us, you accepted it not as a human word, but as it actually is, the word of God, which is indeed at work in you who believe. (1 Thess. 2:13)

For you have been born again, not of perishable seed, but of imperishable, through the living and enduring word of God. (1 Peter 1:23)

The Truth

The Bible is a window into heaven, revealing the purposes of God through the words and emotions of the characters and writers of the sixty-six books that make up the Word of God. When we read the Bible, we're allowed to look longingly through that window. The Bible is also bread to the hungry Christian. It sustains us in every circumstance. If we allow God's Word to shape our lives, we can overcome the troubles that rob us of joy. *Live the Word and be happy.*

Tell Yourself the Truth

"I was born again by believing God's Word, and now the Word lives in me and is at work in me even when I'm unaware of it. I trust fully in God's Word and am not moved by outer circumstances. The Word is my shield in every situation. The Word is my counselor, my comforter, and my instructor. God's Word brings human reasoning to no effect. Through his Word, I overcome the evil one. With the Word dwelling in me and my reliance on what God has said, I cannot be defeated. The more I feast on the Word of God, the more it builds up my spirit. The Word is my anchor. It supports me, rescues me, and changes me day by day."

Pray the Promise

God, I want to know more of your Word! I want you to reveal more of yourself to me as I turn its pages, as I allow its words to permeate my spirit. Continue, Lord, to reveal even more of your precious promises to me so that I might live more consistently in line with your will.

∽

"The Scriptures were not given to increase our knowledge but to change our lives."

— D. L. MOODY

I Live a Life Full of Blessings

The Truth according to God's Word

The LORD will send a blessing on your barns and on everything you put your hand to. The LORD your God will bless you in the land he is giving you. (Deut. 28:8)

May your blessing be on your people. (Ps. 3:8)

"Blessed are those who keep my ways." (Prov. 8:32)

Praise be to the God and Father of our Lord Jesus Christ, who has blessed us in the heavenly realms with every spiritual blessing in Christ. (Eph. 1:3)

The Truth

Inherent in the idea of God "blessing" a person is that the result will be happiness—and indeed that's the case. But this is a happiness from within that comes from God giving us himself as a blessing. And the wonderful thing is that God is a God who *delights* in giving himself to his people. We were built for knowing and loving God.

When we accept by faith God's presence in our lives, we are blessed with happiness.

Not only does God delight in blessing us, but he wants to give a blessing that *exceeds* our expectations. Indeed, in Christ, God has "blessed us in the heavenly realms with every spiritual blessing." We live a blessed life. May God grant us the eyes to see just how blessed we are.

Tell Yourself the Truth

"I am a blessed person! God *delights* to pour his blessings on me. He has redeemed me in order to show me his blessing. He has given me himself that I might be blessed. He has blessed me with his riches so that I can benefit others around me. I am blessed in the heavenly realms with every spiritual blessing in Christ. As I live out my earthly life, those spiritual blessings impact everything I do. Whatever I put my hand to in my walk with him is blessed of God because it originates in God. Because of God's blessing, I cannot fail in life. That's his promise!"

Pray the Promise

Lord, please know that you and you alone are the chief blessing in my life. Nothing else satisfies me like you do. Praise you for revealing yourself and your salvation to me. Wonderful, you are! What a blessed person I am! Thank you, thank you, thank you!

⌒

"However many blessings we expect from God, his infinite liberality will always exceed all our wishes and our thoughts."

— JOHN CALVIN

God Has Drawn the **Boundaries** of My Life

The Truth according to God's Word

Whether you turn to the right or to the left, your ears will hear a voice behind you, saying, "This is the way; walk in it." (Isa. 30:21)

All things are lawful for me, but all things are not helpful. (1 Cor. 6:12 NKJV)

The Truth

We live in an age that dislikes boundaries, yet boundaries are safety barriers that keep us within God's will. Happy are we when we recognize a boundary God has set in place for our own good. And what area of our lives *doesn't* need boundaries — our thought-life? Our relationships? Our time? Our money? Our sexual desires? Yes, all these and more need boundaries. And for each one, God gives us a conscience with which to stake out his boundary. Violate your conscience as formed by God's Word and you violate his boundary for you. Look for God's boundaries in your life. They're there because he loves you.

Tell Yourself the Truth

"Without boundaries, my thoughts and steps wander where they shouldn't go. For that reason, God has set personal boundaries for me. These are lines that I dare not cross, because to do so would endanger me physically, emotionally, or spiritually. Boundaries do not limit my happiness; they enlarge it by keeping me away from the sources of unhappiness. I love the boundaries God has set for me and appreciate God's restraining power that keeps me within those lines as I walk in faith. May God give me more boundaries as he deems necessary. They keep me safe."

Pray the Promise

Thank you, God, for knowing ahead of time that I would need certain boundaries in my life. Some boundaries you've revealed to me through bitter experience as I went places I shouldn't go, hung out with people who led me astray, or did stupid things that only served to reveal how much I need your boundaries. Lord, please continue to make clear to me when I need a new boundary in a certain area of my life. I will be watching, Lord.

∽

"Boundaries are to protect life, not to limit pleasures."

— EDWIN LOUIS COLE

This **Broken Relationship** Hurts My Heart

The Truth according to God's Word

The LORD is close to the brokenhearted
  and saves those who are crushed in spirit. (Ps. 34:18)

He heals the brokenhearted
  and binds up their wounds. (Ps. 147:3)

"Your Father knows what you need before you ask him." (Matt. 6:8)

The Truth

It's very hard to lose a love or a trusted friend. Especially if the breakup wasn't amicable. Harsh words, hurt feelings, and bitter tears are all part of the pain when someone leaves a relationship that was thought to be permanent. But God knows what's going on. Not just what you see, but what he sees that you don't see. If you're willing to go to the places God has for you and do the things God has for you, then this breakup might be for the best. Oh, it doesn't feel that way now and may not for a long time, but time is on your side. Cry some more, then let the tears dry and thank God that he knows what you need right now, even before you ask him. He is waiting to heal your broken heart and bind your wounds. Yes, he is very, very near to you right now. That's his promise. You do have a future beyond this loss. That's his promise too.

Tell Yourself the Truth

"This pain hurts. I feel like the bottom has fallen out of everything. But I'm going to stand up straight, pray for healing, and get on with my life. God knows and God heals. I will not be in this pain forever. I know God's loving plan for me had to include the end of this relationship. Therefore, I resolve to look ahead, not back to what I once had with this person. What I had, I'm now exchanging for something even better, as yet unknown to me. God will reveal it in his time."

Pray the Promise

Father, I don't know why this relationship had to end, but it did. You know all the reasons, many of which are hidden from me. I know that as I trust you and let this relationship truly go—without bitterness or blame—you will take me where you want me to be. Speed the healing, Lord. Help me get far enough along so that I don't look back and renew the pain.

↝

"It is wonderful what miracles God works in wills that are utterly surrendered to Him. He turns hard things into easy, and bitter things into sweet."

—HANNAH WHITALL SMITH

Let Me Come Away with You, Lord — I'm So **Burned Out!**

The Truth according to God's Word

"Come to me, all you who are weary and burdened, and I will give you rest." (Matt. 11:28)

Because so many people were coming and going that they did not even have a chance to eat, he said to them, "Come with me by yourselves to a quiet place and get some rest." (Mark 6:31)

Don't burn out; keep yourselves fueled and aflame. (Rom. 12:11 MSG)

The Truth

It's easy to get overextended these days. Family activities, jobs, schoolwork, friendships, computer time—an excess of attention to any of these things can lead to burnout. And often the result of burnout is that we feel finished. Done. Used up—never to be valuable to God or man again. But Jesus knows what to do about burnout. First, we come *to* him for rest. Then we come *with* him to a quiet place where we can rest. Some people feel guilty when they rest, like they ought to be jumping up and doing the next thing on their list. In reality, the next thing they need to do is learn how to rest. That may mean shutting the computer down for a few days, perhaps going away to some location where rest is possible, or just staying quietly at home. Find a place where you and Jesus can be quiet together. And then when you've rested, you will come back "fueled and aflame," ready to go. Allow your life to be measured, steady, not rushed. Find God's pace for you instead of resuming that same rat-race pace that *always* burns you out.

Tell Yourself the Truth

"I must have a break. I've put all the energy I have into my life's duties, and I just can't go one more day. First, I will quiet my soul. I will shut down all the things that have burned me out so badly. Then I will rest and pray and simply be with Jesus, hearing his wisdom for my life, letting him prioritize my activities. As I become refreshed and return to my life with new energy, I will promise not to allow so many activities in my life that I once again burn out. A balanced, measured life—that's my goal."

Pray the Promise

Lord, you've seen what my life is like. Help me stand strong against the pressing duties that burn me out. Help me learn to say, "No, I'm sorry, I can't take that on right now." Help me, Lord, to order my life by assigning a high, medium, or low priority to all the stuff I must do. Be with me while I rest awhile with you. Teach me how to be truly quiet. Help me still my soul. Bring me into that measured life I desire.

⁓

"You're through. Finished. Burned out. Used up. You've been re-placed ... forgotten. That's a lie!"

— CHARLES SWINDOLL

Children Are a Gift from God

The Truth according to God's Word

May your deeds be shown to your servants,
    your splendor to their children. (Ps. 90:16)

Children are a heritage from the LORD,
    offspring a reward from him.
    Like arrows in the hands of a warrior
    are children born in one's youth. (Ps. 127:3–4)

Jesus said, "Let the little children come to me, and do not hinder them, for the kingdom of heaven belongs to such as these." (Matt. 19:14)

The Truth

Children are a blessing from God. They are our spiritual arrows that we send into the future to keep the faith alive. We must never neglect the duties of influencing our children in the way they should go. If we have failed as parents, we can start now to correct that neglect. If our children are now adults and not walking with God, we can—and must—still pray and believe for their future and never give up hope. Many a parent can relate how

God brought a wayward adult child back to the faith. No, never give up on your children, young or old. Show your children the splendor of the Lord our God. We are the visible presence of the invisible God to our children.

Tell Yourself the Truth

"My children are a blessing to me. God gave these children to me to pray for, to watch over, and to instruct in his ways. I will look at these precious children through God's eyes and see his expectation for their lives. I will believe for great things from them. I will be as kind to them as my heavenly Father is to me. In truth, they are as much my teachers, sent from God, as I am theirs. Most of all, I will show them God's splendor."

Pray the Promise

Lord, thank you for the children in my life. May I be faithful in revealing your splendor to them. May my children walk in your ways. When they err, bring them back quickly and firmly so they won't wander again. May each one be an arrow you send into the future to be a blessing to the next generation. When I'm gone, watch over my children. Keep them covered, Lord. Keep them safe in the shadow of your wings.

~

"You may speak but a word to a child, and in that child there may be slumbering a noble heart which shall stir the Christian church in years to come."

— CHARLES SPURGEON

I Can Find Contentment In Every **Circumstance**

The Truth according to God's Word

We know that in all things God works for the good of those who love him, who have been called according to his purpose. (Rom. 8:28)

I have learned to be content whatever the circumstances. (Phil. 4:11)

Give thanks in all circumstances; for this is God's will for you in Christ Jesus. (1 Thess. 5:18)

The Truth

Circumstances happen. God is never absent during the direst circumstances. When we trust him, *all* our circumstances will work together for our good. The secret is to keep our eyes on him, not on our circumstances.

Tell Yourself the Truth

"God is never surprised by my circumstances. He is sovereign and sees my every situation as a pathway to the future he has planned for me. Even adverse circumstances are turned by God into stepping-stones to my destiny. I give thanks in all circumstances, knowing that God orchestrates them all for my eventual good. I trust him with even the hardest circumstances in my life. God works on my behalf through every situation. There is no circumstance that can diminish my faith. There is no circumstance that will not make me stronger if I meet it with faith in God. God sees. He knows. He understands. He is always moving behind the scenes."

Pray the Promise

Father, you are Lord of my every circumstance. Even when circumstances seem against me, you are there. I believe you and trust you as I pray and watch you arrange the circumstances of my life. In each case, I look for your purpose in working all things to my good.

~

"If we cannot believe God when circumstances seem to be against us, we do not believe him at all."

— CHARLES SPURGEON

God Gives Me **Clarity of Mind** to Unravel Tangled Situations

The Truth according to God's Word

But we have the mind of Christ. (1 Cor. 2:16)

For God has not given us a spirit of fear, but of power and of love and of a sound mind.
   (2 Tim. 1:7 NKJV)

The Truth

God wants us to think clearly. A muddled mind is of no use to God. His Spirit allows us to focus our minds squarely on the issues at hand. Just as Jesus kept his focus not on the cross ahead of him but on what it would secure for us, the ones he loves, so too we can focus not on our troubles but, with clearness of thought, keep our eyes and minds on him.

Tell Yourself the Truth

"God has gifted me with a wonderful brain. And by his promise, I have the mind of Christ; therefore I can think clearly and reasonably without confusion. I am able to make sound decisions, trusting that God will work through any decision I make in faith and in accordance with his Word. My clear mind thinks things through with God-directed reasoning. I come to the conclusions I should as I think with the mind of Christ and am led by the Holy Spirit living within me. I do not let misleading emotions take me off track. My mind is active, not passive; creative, not stodgy; productive, not lazy; God-centered, not problem-driven. My mind is a glorious gift of God, able to figure out the next step to take in any situation."

Pray the Promise

Thank you, Lord, for a clear, disciplined, orderly mind. In the natural, my thoughts are often scattered and useless. But you give me the ability to think as I should. You bring solutions to problems to my mind. You give me discernment in troublesome situations and insight into potential disasters before they happen. You provide your Holy Spirit to guide and direct me. Lord, I consider my mind to be a gift from you and a tool for you.

⌒

"Ah! dear friend, you little know the possibilities which are in you."

— CHARLES SPURGEON

I Have the **Compassion** of Christ and Share It with Those in Need

The Truth according to God's Word

Be kind and compassionate to one another, forgiving each other, just as in Christ God forgave you. (Eph. 4:32)

Therefore, as God's chosen people, holy and dearly loved, clothe yourselves with compassion. (Col. 3:12)

All of you, be like-minded, be sympathetic, love one another, be compassionate and humble. (1 Peter 3:8)

The Truth

God's people are a compassionate people. Just as God is "full of compassion," so must we be. We give our time, money, and prayers to those in need. We give our presence when that will meet a need. God has no hands and no feet to use but ours in reaching those who need compassion. May we always respond with compassionate hearts to the needs of others that God sets before us.

Tell Yourself the Truth

"God has shown tender compassion for me over and over again. And because of his compassion for me, I am tender and compassionate toward others. I allow God to care for other people through me. I bring his compassion to the hurting as God alerts me to the needs of those around me. I respond to needs with kindness and whatever resources I have. By my compassion, I become the hands and feet of Christ to others in their sin or pain, offering hope, redemption, and wholeness. Just as God has given me, so do I give to others. God's compassion finds an outlet through me."

Pray the Promise

Here I am, Lord; send me! Allow me to be your hands, feet, and mouth to those in need. I will be a comforter to the hurting, a messenger of good news to those who are lost. I will never look at people in need — no matter what their need — as somehow undeserving of my compassion.

⌣

"How far you go in life depends on your being tender with the young, compassionate with the aged, sympathetic with the striving, and tolerant of the weak and strong. Because someday in your life you will have been all of these."

— GEORGE WASHINGTON CARVER

There Is No **Condemnation** for Those Who Are in Christ Jesus — and That Includes *Me*

The Truth according to God's Word

For God did not send his Son into the world to condemn the world, but to save the world through him. Whoever believes in him is not condemned, but whoever does not believe stands condemned already because they have not believed in the name of God's one and only Son. (John 3:17 – 18)

Jesus ... asked her, "Woman, where are they? Has no one condemned you?"

"No one, sir," she said.

"Then neither do I condemn you," Jesus declared. "Go now and leave your life of sin." (John 8:10 – 11)

Therefore, there is now no condemnation for those who are in Christ Jesus. (Rom. 8:1)

The Truth

Feelings of condemnation in the Christian don't square with God's acceptance of us as being in Christ. Being in Christ means to be forever free from condemnation. The enemy, however, still seeks to condemn us and thus weaken us. He well knows that a Christian with a condemning conscience lacks power.

However, Christ has set us free from our guilt—the only reason for anyone to feel condemnation. Freedom from guilt is part of our inheritance as Christians. Because of Christ, we can walk boldly through life with a clear conscience. All our sins have been fully dealt with at the cross. This we must believe—and live.

Tell Yourself the Truth

"God does not condemn me—he loves me. In Christ, I'm free from all condemnation. No feelings of shame have any part in me, for Christ has taken away my shame. I resist and turn away any sense of condemnation that either Satan or my own emotions try to place on me. I know that with my sins gone forever, the enemy has no grounds for condemning me. I am righteous in Christ. Never again will I allow false guilt or condemnation to cloud my relationship with God. Never."

Pray the Promise

Lord, I thank you that I may hear the same words from you as did the woman taken in adultery: "Neither do I condemn you. Go now and leave your life of sin." Knowing I am forever free from condemnation gives me joy.

⌒

"Faith cancels all that is past, and there is no condemnation to thee."
— JOHN WESLEY

God Is a **Creative** God, and I Am Made in His Image

The Truth according to God's Word

Then Moses said to the Israelites, "See, the LORD has chosen Bezalel son of Uri, the son of Hur, of the tribe of Judah, and he has filled him with the Spirit of God, with wisdom, with understanding, with knowledge and with all kinds of skills—to make artistic designs for work in gold, silver and bronze, to cut and set stones, to work in wood and to engage in all kinds of artistic crafts. And he has given both him and Oholiab son of Ahisamak, of the tribe of Dan, the ability to teach others. He has filled them with skill to do all kinds of work as engravers, designers, embroiderers in blue, purple and scarlet yarn and fine linen, and weavers—all of them skilled workers and designers." (Ex. 35:30–35)

Do you see someone skilled in their work?
They will serve before kings. (Prov. 22:29)

Whatever you do, work at it with all your heart, as working for the Lord, not for human masters, since you know that you will receive an inheritance from the Lord as a reward. (Col. 3:23–24)

The Truth

God is the ultimate creative being. Has there ever been a man or woman who has not gasped at some great work of God in nature—an astonishingly beautiful sunset or the intricacy of a sparkling spiderweb? Even our human bodies are evidences of his creative genius. And we, being made in his image, are called to be great creators, each in our own way—whether, for example, as an artist, writer, poet, seamstress, chef, designer, or, as was Jesus, a carpenter. (Wouldn't you love to see some piece of carpentry Jesus built?)

As with all the gifts we have from God, humility must be our response to these trusts he has given us. Every Christian, deep down, knows the true source of his or her gifts.

If you say, "I have no such creative talent," I'd encourage you to pray about that. I suspect you do have a gift and either don't recognize it as such, and thus possibly minimize it in your own mind, or haven't yet discovered it. Many gifted people don't appreciate their giftedness until later in life. Pray, keep watching, and don't be afraid to step out and experiment. God has something in mind to release your latent talents.

Tell Yourself the Truth

"In bearing the image of God, I, like him, am creative. He has deposited in me the ability to fashion creations unique to my talents. I have more creative ability in me than I can even imagine. These gifts are a trust from God that I steward with great care. I do not waste them or use them for ignoble purposes. My artistic life is a continual tapping into the creative one whose creativity knows no bounds. His ability to create beauty out of nothing inspires me to create works that are worthy of the talent he has given me. My goal is to bring glory to God through my gifts, not glory to myself. No matter the level of success I have in my artistic endeavors, I vow always to reflect all the praise back to him."

Pray the Promise

What wonderful creative gifts you've given me, Lord! And all are just a mere iota of the creativity you possess. May I have more, Lord? I ask that you multiply my talents just as you multiplied the fish and loaves for the hungry crowd. May my most creative days be ahead of me, and may the creative waters continue to flow through me until my last day.

∽

"God gives us gifts, graces, and natural talents, not for our own use, but that we may render them to him."

— MADAME JEANNE GUYON

I Do Not Fear **Death**, for I Know God Will Receive Me

The Truth according to God's Word

Precious in the sight of the LORD
 is the death of his faithful servants. (Ps. 116:15)

"I am the resurrection and the life. The one who believes in me will live, even though they die; and whoever lives by believing in me will never die." (John 11:25 – 26)

For to me, to live is Christ and to die is gain. (Phil. 1:21)

The Truth

For the Christian, death is an entrance into an even greater life — and the presence of the Lord. It has been well described as walking from one room into another. We need have no fear of death. When the lab tests result in a bad report, we pray for health, but all the same, we know that our final home is secured for us by Christ and that our eventual death is precious in God's sight. There is, then, nothing to fear about that coming day. We can rest from worry and from fear.

Tell Yourself the Truth

"I do not fear my death. How can I fear that which draws me into my heavenly home where I will continually be in God's presence and experience pure joy? When the Lord calls, I will go gladly and peacefully into his presence. I believe God has that day set aside for me just as if it were a date with a loved one. And this is a date I long to keep. But meanwhile I live fully in this life, serving him and loving him with all my being. Until that precious day does arrive, nothing fatal can touch me. I am safe from all harm."

Pray the Promise

Lord, there is much work for me to do here. But your calendar is more accurate than mine. When you call me, I will be overjoyed to come into your presence forever. On a day known only to you, we will meet face-to-face, never to part.

∽

"Are you afraid to die? Remember that for a child of God, death is only a passing through to a wonderful new world."

— CORRIE TEN BOOM

God Gives Me Wisdom for the Many **Decisions** I Must Make

The Truth according to God's Word

I will instruct you and teach you in the way you should go;
   I will counsel you with my loving eye on you. (Ps. 32:8)

Show me the way I should go,
   for to you I entrust my life. (Ps. 143:8)

If any of you lacks wisdom, you should ask God, who gives generously to all without finding fault, and it will be given to you. (James 1:5)

The Truth

During our lifetime, we are faced with many decisions, some major, some minor. But in every case, a decision made in faith, trusting God for the results, will work out better than a decision based on doubt and fear. When we pray for wisdom, we must believe God answers that prayer. Sometimes we don't understand why we're making the decision we're making, and sometimes we don't see the immediate results we expect, but time will reveal that a faithful decision made in accordance with God's leading in prayer was the right one.

Tell Yourself the Truth

"When faced with a decision, I seek God's mind on the matter, ask for wisdom, and believe God gives it generously. Then I act on the decision, trusting God with the results. I don't fear making the wrong choice, because I choose in faith, not with a double mind. God will make the right choice clear to me even if clarity only comes later."

Pray the Promise

God, I need your help making the right decisions. I've made some poor ones in the past, and I've learned a good lesson: what looks right to me isn't always right to you. I pray that when I'm facing a decision and some important factors are unknown to me, you will reveal them to me. Give me clarity, Lord, as I decide. Give me wise counselors whose opinions I can trust. Guide me from your Word too, Lord. May all my decisions be faith-filled decisions, not wavering but trusting you.

↜

"When I am anxious about decisions I have to make about the future, I battle unbelief with the promise, 'I will instruct you and teach you in the way which you should go; I will counsel you with My eye upon you.'"

— JOHN PIPER

When I Suffer from Depression, Even Then God Is with Me

The Truth according to God's Word

You, Lord, are my lamp;
  the Lord turns my darkness into light. (2 Sam. 22:29)

Why, my soul, are you downcast?
  Why so disturbed within me?
Put your hope in God,
  for I will yet praise him,
    my Savior and my God. (Ps. 43:5)

The Lord upholds all who fall
  and lifts up all who are bowed down. (Ps. 145:14)

The Truth

Unless due to a physical cause, depression is a result of the temporary inability to see ourselves and our situation through God's eyes. When, by faith, we see as God sees, our depression can be replaced by joy. God lifts our head when it is bowed down in depression. He allows us to see as he sees.

Tell Yourself the Truth

"Men and women in the Bible—Job, David, Moses, Jonah—suffered from depression. But God came to their rescue. He rescues me too when I'm bowed down with crushing depression."

"When depressed, I do six things:

1. I determine if there's a physical cause by talking to my doctor.
2. I reject any satanic source of my depression, whether these are "fiery darts" in the form of depressing thoughts or links to occult practices in my past.
3. I deliberately, by an act of faith, begin to praise God. I *will* to rejoice. I *will* to abandon my sorrow and sadness in favor of praise. Even when my emotions don't follow, yet I still praise him.
4. I verbally name one by one the good things in my life and thank God for each of these blessings.
5. I begin to pray for others who I know need God's help.
6. I turn to the book of Psalms and read aloud my favorite verses. I choose a strong verse against depression and claim it as my own, repeating it aloud as necessary.

"The combination of renouncing the source of my depression, thanking and praising God, and trusting in his Word enables me to renew my mind and make depression a thing of the past."

Pray the Promise

God, how I hate depression! It cripples me. I'm not good when under that dark cloud. But, God, you lift my depression as I choose to worship you in spite of every depressing impulse that rails against praise. I choose verses from your Word to combat the riptide that pulls me out to sea. Lord, save me as I walk on the rough sea waters toward you!

∽

"The secret of joy is not to wait until you feel happy, but to rise, by an act of faith, out of the depression which is dragging you down and begin to praise God as an act of choice."

— A. B. SIMPSON

God Has Called Me to a **Destiny** That Only I Can Fulfill

The Truth according to God's Word

We are God's handiwork, created in Christ Jesus to do good works, which God prepared in advance for us to do. (Eph. 2:10)

But you, keep your head in all situations, endure hardship, do the work of an evangelist, discharge all the duties of your ministry. (2 Tim. 4:5)

The Truth

God has a plan to use *you* for his high purposes. Every Christian has a destiny: an assignment from God—a mission to accomplish. Our unique task was prepared for us in eternity past and awaits our completion. Our response is to pursue our work with confidence that God has fully equipped us and empowered us to do what he wants of us.

If you think you're in such a lowly and obscure place that God cannot use you, consider Henry Varley's life-changing words to meager shoe salesman D. L. Moody: "The world has yet to see what God can do with and for and through and in a man who is fully and wholly consecrated to him."

You have a call on your life equal to that of the great nineteenth-century evangelist D. L. Moody, Billy Graham, or Susanna Wesley, mother of those historic men of God, John and Charles Wesley.

Embrace your destiny with joy and anticipation!

Tell Yourself the Truth

"I have a calling on my life — a destiny and an assignment uniquely fitted to me by God. I embrace with joy the divine assignment given to me by God. On the day of my death, God will have accomplished all the mighty deeds through me that he ordained since eternity past. I press ahead in prayer and thanksgiving, discovering the gifts God has equipped me with for my assignment. I am privileged to be chosen for this unique task. Glory to God!"

Pray the Promise

God, you have a work for me that only I can do. Not only do I accept this work, but I eagerly pursue it. I watch for you to reveal new aspects of it, to change it if necessary, and to reveal it if I'm not already aware of it. Be it a large work or a small work, it is what you have for me, and I praise you for it.

∽

"We are made for larger ends than Earth can encompass. Oh, let us be true to our exalted destiny."

— CATHERINE BOOTH

God Will Help Me Relate to the **Difficult People** in My Life

The Truth according to God's Word

A gentle answer turns away wrath,
>   but a harsh word stirs up anger....
>   The soothing tongue is a tree of life,
>   but a perverse tongue crushes the spirit. (Prov. 15:1, 4)

"But I tell you, love your enemies and pray for those who persecute you, that you may be children of your Father in heaven.... If you love those who love you, what reward will you get?" (Matt. 5:44–46)

Speaking the truth in love, we will grow to become in every respect the mature body of him who is the head, that is, Christ. (Eph. 4:15)

The Truth

Everyone has at least one difficult person in his or her life. But when we realize that God has called us to love the unlovely — the difficult person — we can do so when we realize that God loved us in our unloveliness — when we were his difficult people.

Tell Yourself the Truth

"I think now of the difficult people in my life. They do get under my skin. They seem to know all the buttons to push. But the truth is that they may have sadnesses, situations, trials that I know nothing about. Their toxicity may be the only way they know how to cope. I will not judge my difficult people. I will show them compassion. I will love them by faith. I will be God's ambassador to those in my life who are the hardest to love. I will also speak the truth to them in love. The outcome is God's. I will do my part by being patient with them and kind to them, and I will turn the other cheek when they verbally abuse me. May God be honored in the results in their lives and in mine."

Pray the Promise

Lord, about my difficult person: Help! *You know how this person affects me. Please give me the right words to say, the compassion to listen, and the patience to bear their negative personality. If they are no longer to be a part of my life due to their destructiveness, I pray you'd show me how to appropriately and kindly separate myself from them. Otherwise, I rely on you for the necessary love and patience. And, Lord, I pray that I may never be someone else's difficult person.*

⌁

"Our Lord has many weak children in his family, many dull pupils in his school, many raw soldiers in his army, many lame sheep in his flock. Yet he bears with them all and casts none away. Happy is that Christian who has learned to do likewise with his brethren."

—J. C. RYLE

Disappointment Means God Will Open Another Door, Not This One

The Truth according to God's Word

Though the fig tree does not bud
and there are no grapes on the vines,
though the olive crop fails
and the fields produce no food,
though there are no sheep in the pen
and no cattle in the stalls,
yet I will rejoice in the LORD,
I will be joyful in God my Savior. (Hab. 3:17 – 18)

" 'Your kingdom come,
your will be done,
on earth as it is in heaven.' " (Matt. 6:10)

The Truth

Disappointment is a human reaction when God zigs and we zag. But through the eyes of faith, we see that his direction was right and ours was wrong. We may very well discover that we zagged because we were wrongly motivated or we looked to fallible people to do certain things and they let us down. Or we may have presumed upon God. Perhaps we have asked him to conform his will to ours rather than making sure our will conformed to his.

The good news is that faith can turn disappointment into God's appointment.

Tell Yourself the Truth

"This disappointment hurts. I feel let down when I expect one thing and another happens. But I will lay aside my own feelings and watch for God's results to come from this present letdown. I will continue to pray and expect God to redeem this disappointing turn of events. By faith, it *will* turn out for the best. This disappointment *will be* God's appointment."

Pray the Promise

Lord, this disappointment is hard to bear. You know what I expected, and now you see how it turned out otherwise. I had prayed about this, Lord, and was not expecting this outcome. Help me to see by faith that this sharp right turn will somehow lead me to the right place — although a place I was not expecting to go. If you are there waiting, it will all be good.

⟿

"There is many a thing which the world calls disappointment, but there is no such word in the dictionary of faith. What to others are disappointments are to believers intimations of the way of God."

— JOHN NEWTON

God Is Still God When Disaster Strikes

The Truth according to God's Word

The blameless spend their days under the LORD's care,
    and their inheritance will endure forever.
    In times of disaster they will not wither. (Ps. 37:18 – 19)

"When you pass through the waters,
    I will be with you;
    and when you pass through the rivers,
    they will not sweep over you.
    When you walk through the fire,
    you will not be burned;
    the flames will not set you ablaze." (Isa. 43:2)

The Truth

Disasters come in all shapes and sizes. Some are personal disasters affecting just us or our families. Others, such as natural disasters — earthquakes, tornadoes, floods, fires — take both a personal toll and a collective toll to all touched by them.

But is God absent when disaster strikes? Are we not to trust God even then? Of course, we must trust — especially during times of disaster. God is not unaware of our plight. He knows and he provides. The apostle Paul was on a ship bound for Rome when a storm arose and threatened to sink the ship. Paul, however, remained confident and told the ship's crew to be courageous. When they finally were shipwrecked on Malta, Paul prayed for the father of the island's chief official, who was then healed. Acts 28:9 tells us the result was "the rest of the sick on the island came and were cured." Out of disaster came an opportunity to help others, to minister in Christ's name. When disaster strikes, take Paul's advice to be courageous; then watch for ways for God to use you in the midst of the turmoil. Paul eventually arrived in Rome. You too will eventually arrive at your good destination. Just stand still, wait, and see God bring you through.

Tell Yourself the Truth

"I don't look for or expect disaster, but if and when it comes, I will fix my hope squarely on God. He will see me through *any* calamity. God is never surprised. He sees when disaster is coming, and he is there for me to lean on when I feel overwhelmed. I run fully into the outstretched arms of God, and though I can't see it now, I remain confident that the outcome of this disaster will work for good. No flood, no tornado, no fire, no earthquake — no disaster of any kind — can come against me that God won't oversee with his watchful eye. During such times, I will trust him fully."

Pray the Promise

Lord, help! I never saw this coming. Now, in the wake of disaster, I cry out to you. Strengthen me! Help me remain calm as I trust in you. If there is a way you plan to use this calamity for my good, may it be so. I will walk by faith, not by sight. I will trust.

"To learn strong faith is to endure great trials. I have learned my faith by standing firm amid severe testings."

— GEORGE MUELLER

God Gives Me **Discernment** in Knowing What to Accept and What to Reject

The Truth according to God's Word

I am your servant; give me discernment
   that I may understand your statutes. (Ps. 119:125)

A discerning person keeps wisdom in view,
   but a fool's eyes wander to the ends of the earth. (Prov. 17:24)

And this is my prayer: that your love may abound more and more in knowledge and depth of insight, so that you may be able to discern what is best and may be pure and blameless for the day of Christ, filled with the fruit of righteousness that comes through Jesus Christ — to the glory and praise of God. (Phil. 1:9 – 11)

The Truth

Discernment is a mark of maturity. Through discernment we understand God's statutes — what he wants from us. Discernment can be likened to reading traffic signs along the road: Stop,

YIELD, SLOW DOWN, BRIDGE MAY BE ICY. All these and more are warnings to the wise. An immature, impulsive person lacks discernment and ignores the markers God puts along life's highway. The discerning person watches for God's signals and obeys them. Such a person easily stays on course.

Tell Yourself the Truth

"I will not follow my fleeting emotions but will discern a matter in the light of God's Word. I trust that God will give me discernment in every situation and will nudge me in my spirit when I'm not discerning rightly. I watch for God's signposts along the way, and I obey them. I listen for the quiet voice of God that helps me discern what is "best and pure and blameless.""

Pray the Promise

God, help me see beyond what my natural eyes see. Let me rightly discern when something that appears right is, instead, wrong. Keep me on the right road, safely obeying your road signs, neither wandering off into the ditch on the left or on the right.

∽

"Discernment is God's call to intercession, never to faultfinding."

— CORRIE TEN BOOM

I Am a Disciple — a **Disciplined** Person

The Truth according to God's Word

Therefore, I urge you, brothers and sisters, in view of God's mercy, to offer your bodies as a living sacrifice, holy and pleasing to God — this is your true and proper worship. (Rom. 12:1)

For the Spirit God gave us does not make us timid, but gives us power, love and self-discipline. (2 Tim. 1:7)

The end of all things is at hand; therefore be self-controlled and sober-minded for the sake of your prayers. (1 Peter 4:7 ESV)

The Truth

God works best through a disciplined person. He is hindered when we are undisciplined in body, thought, or speech. But God's discipline is not rigid and uncomfortable. We can easily control ourselves when we walk in his Spirit, for the Spirit he has given us is one of self-discipline.

Tell Yourself the Truth

"I am a disciple of Christ. Therefore I assume the responsibility of being a *disciplined* follower of Christ. Through his Spirit, I curb my own wants and appetites in favor of what God wants. My unruly flesh is subdued and obedient to carry out the plans of God for me. God-inspired discipline allows me to be used by God to the maximum; therefore I embrace discipline as a gift from God."

Pray the Promise

Heavenly Father, show the way to keep my body, mind, and spirit disciplined. I commit my way to you, asking you to use my disciplined self to achieve all you have for me.

⬿

"Discipline, for the Christian, begins with the body. We have only one. It is this body that is the primary material given to us for sacrifice. We cannot give our hearts to God and keep our bodies for ourselves."

— ELISABETH ELLIOT

I Believe God Has Set Up Divine Appointments

The Truth according to God's Word

Then [Abraham's servant] prayed, "LORD, God of my master Abraham, make me successful today, and show kindness to my master Abraham. See, I am standing beside this spring, and the daughters of the townspeople are coming out to draw water. May it be that when I say to a young woman, 'Please let down your jar that I may have a drink,' and she says, 'Drink, and I'll water your camels too' — let her be the one you have chosen for your servant Isaac. By this I will know that you have shown kindness to my master."

Before he had finished praying, Rebekah came out with her jar on her shoulder. (Gen. 24:12–15)

The steps of a good man are ordered by the LORD,
    And He delights in his way. (Ps. 37:23 NKJV)

LORD, you are my God;
    I will exalt you and praise your name,
    for in perfect faithfulness
    you have done wonderful things,
    things planned long ago. (Isa. 25:1)

The Truth

God is always setting up divine appointments for us. The Bible is chock full of divine appointments, whether it's the dramatic story of Isaac and Rebecca in the Old Testament or Jesus' encounter with the woman at the well in the New Testament. Those kinds of appointments still happen today. We need only to open our eyes and be aware.

Tell Yourself the Truth

"God has divine appointments arranged for me from the beginning of time. These divine appointments move me ahead in my assignment on earth. However, if I'm not aware, I may miss these appointed times. Daily I will watch for ways God wants to use me by the encounters he sets up with other people. In each case, I know God will show me what to say and do."

Pray the Promise

Lord, order my steps each day. Bring me to the right person or place where I have an appointment arranged by you. Perhaps the appointment is for the good of the person I'm meeting, or perhaps it's for my good. Eitehr way, direct my steps, O God.

～

"I will charge my soul to believe and wait for Him, and will follow His providence, and not go before it, nor stay behind it."

— SAMUEL RUTHERFORD

Doubt Is the Enemy of Faith. With God's Help I Can Overcome My Doubts and Press On in Faith

The Truth according to God's Word

When [Peter] saw the wind, he was afraid and, beginning to sink, cried out, "Lord, save me!" Immediately Jesus reached out his hand and caught him. "You of little faith," he said, "why did you doubt?" And when they climbed into the boat, the wind died down. (Matt. 14:30–32)

[The disciples] were startled and frightened, thinking they saw a ghost. [Jesus] said to them, "Why are you troubled, and why do doubts rise in your minds? Look at my hands and my feet. It is I myself! Touch me and see; a ghost does not have flesh and bones, as you see I have." (Luke 24:37–39)

The Truth

As with the disciples, especially Peter and Thomas, doubts arise in our minds from time to time. But must we therefore accept these doubts as friends, or may we show them the door and turn our thoughts to the steady truth of God's Word? We know that God wants us to have faith and that doubt is the enemy of faith. God would therefore have us feed our faith (through his Word, prayer, and fellowship with others) and starve our doubts (by avoiding negative or evil influences in our lives).

Tell Yourself the Truth

"God knows my doubts. And yet every time I've begun to sink in the waters, as did Peter, I've cried out 'Lord, save me!' And he has. He has proven himself faithful to me over and over again. So once more, I cast my doubts on him and ask him to summon me to walk toward him across the waters. And, sure enough, just as Peter found out once he was back in the boat, the wind *does* die down. As for me, I choose to believe the wind will die down while I'm yet walking on the water by faith, not looking at the storm of doubt determined to plunge me into the water. Faith is, after all, stronger than doubt. Faith moves mountains; doubt builds them."

Pray the Promise

Lord, I will refuse to entertain doubts about you, your Word, or my future. All is in your very capable hands. Even when my faith is the size of a mustard seed, it will see me through if I put it to good use and do not let doubt uproot it. Lord, I do believe.

‟

"I believe that the happiest of Christians and the truest of Christians are those who never dare to doubt God, but who take his Word simply as it stands, and believe it, and ask no questions, just feeling assured that if God has said it, it will be so."

— CHARLES SPURGEON

God Frees Me from Emotional Dependency on Others

The Truth according to God's Word

Fear of man will prove to be a snare,
But whoever trusts in the LORD is kept safe. (Prov. 29:25)

They loved human praise more than praise from God. (John 12:43)

In Christ you have been brought to fullness. (Col. 2:10)

The Truth

There is a vast difference between what we need from other people and what we need that only God can give. We often mistake the two. We look for the wrong kind of affirmation from other people, when what we're really signaling with our desperate emotional longings is, "God, I need you in a far deeper way."

Instead of saying those words and looking to God, who is only too ready and even eager to fill that fierce emotional longing, we become people pleasers. We try to do, say, or comply with what we perceive will make others give us the attention we think will fill that emotional longing. But only God can meet that need. And the moment we realize this is the moment our wounds can begin to heal, our stress will lessen, and even our physical health can benefit.

The alternative is to keep chasing the wind in the form of the acceptance and applause of other people. Even if we should receive the acclaim we seek, it remains a very hollow substitute for the acceptance and applause of God—the one who has brought us to fullness. Our expectation must be of him, not of others, to satisfy our longings.

Tell Yourself the Truth

"I seek only the praise that comes from God, not the people around me. I do not manipulate or try to control the way other people think about me. I answer only to God. He meets my emotional needs as I make them known to him. He comforts me and supplies the emotional support no other person can give. God is always enough, but when he sends messengers of hope in the form of friends and other people, I accept them as gifts from God, never allowing them to take God's place in providing the acceptance I need and that only he can give."

Pray the Promise

Father God, I lean on you for acceptance. There are times when I'm tempted to find someone—anyone, to meet my emotional needs. I know that you use other people to love and care for me, but I also know that only you can fill me. I find true emotional health in grasping your full acceptance of me. Thank you for loving me the way you do. You love me totally.

"No soul can be really at rest until it has given up all dependence on everything else and has been forced to depend on the Lord alone. As long as our expectation is from other things, nothing but disappointment awaits us."

— HANNAH WHITALL SMITH

My **Emotions** *Express* How I Feel; They Don't *Determine* How I Feel

The Truth according to God's Word

Have mercy on me, LORD, for I am faint;
    heal me, LORD, for my bones are in agony.
    My soul is in deep anguish.
    How long, LORD, how long?
    Turn, LORD, and deliver me;
    save me because of your unfailing love. . . .
    I am worn out from my groaning. (Ps. 6:2–4, 6)

Better a patient person than a warrior,
    one with self-control than one who takes a city. (Prov. 16:32)

Fools give full vent to their rage,
    but the wise bring calm in the end. (Prov. 29:11)

The Truth

Our Christian walk is too easily swayed by how we feel. When we're feeling good, we feel spiritually fit. All is well in our Christian world. But then when something happens to bring our emotions down or make us angry, if we're not careful, we can allow those feelings to influence our fellowship with God. We may even think God is displeased with us when our emotions are at an ebb. But the truth is that our emotions are not an accurate gauge of our spiritual condition. If we have trusted Christ, we are his. *Period.* And when our emotions try to tell us he is disappointed in us, and that's why we feel so drained, that's just plain wrong. Our emotional state has zero effect on our standing with God. *Zero.* We are in Christ and in Christ we will stay. Don't let your emotions rob you of your fellowship with God. Praise him when you're happy and praise him when you're sad. Take control of your emotions rather than giving them full vent and you'll find that your emotions will follow your decision to praise him.

Tell Yourself the Truth

"My emotions are not a reliable measure of my fellowship with God; therefore I will not allow any emotion to rule my spiritual life. I will be a person with steady, reliable emotions that express how I feel but not determine how I feel. My emotions must follow my will in choosing to praise God; they must not be the leader of my spirit."

Pray the Promise

Thank you, Father, for my emotions. What a great provision to allow us to express a variety of responses to life. But, oh, how deceptive feelings can be when they're allowed to rule my life. God, keep me emotionally steady. Remind me during "down" times that your love for me is as strong as ever.

"Believe God's love and power more than you believe your own feelings and experiences. Your rock is Christ, and it is not the rock that ebbs and flows, but the sea."

— SAMUEL RUTHERFORD

God Gives Me **Employment** and Favor on the Job

The Truth according to God's Word

Those who work their land will have abundant food,
   but those who chase fantasies have no sense. (Prov. 12:11)

Whatever your hand finds to do, do it with all your might. (Eccl. 9:10)

Anyone who has been stealing must steal no longer, but must work, doing something useful with their own hands, that they may have something to share with those in need. (Eph. 4:28)

The Truth

Work is good. We are all called to be laborers at some meaningful task. Knowing that God has called us to work for him is the key to pressing on with our daily tasks without burning out. If we have a job, we should be thankful and do our best. If we need a job, we should pray and pursue work that pleases us, trusting God for the very job he has reserved for us. If we are unhappy in our job, we can also pray for God to move us on and bring us to a job we love, asking him to open the right doors.

Tell Yourself the Truth

"My job is God's gift to me. I will be good at what I do. I will give my employer the best I have to give, working as unto the Lord. I trust that when I'm finished with this present job—whether sooner or later—God will move me where he wants me next. I do not fear layoffs or unemployment. When this job ends, it's with God's consent. God is my source of income, and he will provide the means for me to prosper at what I do."

Pray the Promise

God, you know my resume. You know the jobs I've held and the job I'd like to have. I pray that you would keep me happy where I am—and grateful for this job—or move me to a better job where I can be more useful and happier. When I'm without a job, I know it's temporary, for your will is for me to work, not be idle. I praise you, Father, for the opportunity to work.

⌒

"This job has been given to me to do. Therefore, it is a gift. Therefore, it is a privilege. Therefore, it is an offering I may make to God. Therefore, it is to be done gladly, if it is done for him. Here, not somewhere else, I may learn God's way. In this job, not in some other, God looks for faithfulness."

—ELISABETH ELLIOT

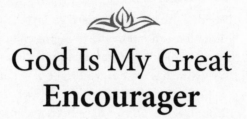

God Is My Great Encourager

The Truth according to God's Word

David encouraged himself in the LORD his God. (1 Sam. 30:6 KJV)

May our Lord Jesus Christ himself and God our Father, who loved us and by his grace gave us eternal encouragement and good hope, encourage your hearts and strengthen you in every good deed and word. (2 Thess. 2:16–17)

The Truth

One of the many reasons God gave us his Word is to encourage us. Through the stories of the many heroes and heroines of the Bible, we see the results of steadfast faith in the midst of often horrible circumstances. When we feel like we can't go on, we can turn to the Bible and read about Noah, Ruth, Job, David, Peter, and many others. We can't possibly be in a worse predicament than they were. And in every case, they prevailed by trusting God in the midst of their discouragement. So must we. And when we are "encouraged in the Lord," as was David, we are duty-bound to encourage those around us. When we encourage others, we're speaking to them with the very words God would say to them.

Tell Yourself the Truth

"Like King David, I must often encourage myself in the Lord, my God. My situation is no more discouraging than what others have lived through. They have prevailed by faith and patience, and so will I. Every life has seasons, and right now I'm in a season where I need to be reminded this won't last forever. Other Christians down through the centuries have been encouraged by our God—and so shall I. The plans God has for me are for good and not for evil, and in God brighter days are ahead for me. This tunnel will soon end."

Pray the Promise

God, will you be my cheerleader in life? I need someone to keep me encouraged when times get rough. Remind me by whispering in my heart that you've seen what is up ahead and everything is going to be okay. Thank you for your Word, which greatly encourages me when I'm low.

∽

"Nothing but encouragement can come to us as we dwell upon the faithful dealing of our heavenly Father in centuries gone by. Faith in God has not saved people from hardships and trials, but it has enabled them to bear tribulations courageously and to emerge victoriously."

— LEE ROBERSON

My **Enemies** Cannot Ruin Me. I Pray for Them and Leave Them in God's Hands

The Truth according to God's Word

Lead me, LORD, in your righteousness
  because of my enemies—
  make your way straight before me. (Ps. 5:8)

I called to the LORD, who is worthy of praise,
  and I have been saved from my enemies. (Ps. 18:3)

"Love your enemies, do good to them, and lend to them without expecting to get anything back. Then your reward will be great, and you will be children of the Most High, because he is kind to the ungrateful and wicked." (Luke 6:35)

The Truth

Our enemies are not really our enemies. We have only one enemy, and he has been defeated at the cross. The flesh and blood enemies we face here on earth are men and women—estranged from

God and in desperate need of rescue, just as we used to be. If God is kind to them by giving them life and offering them repentance, isn't it worth our being kind to them so that we may be called children of the Most High?

Tell Yourself the Truth

"I don't hate my enemies. By faith, I love them and pray for them. When they say or do harmful things, I consider that they're acting according to their fallen nature — just as I once did. I choose to do good to my enemies, so that they might see how God thinks of them in spite of their rebellion against him. Prayer and love active in good works and kindness will undo the fiercest of my enemies."

Pray the Promise

Lord, you know who my enemies are. They have chosen me; I have not chosen them. I would befriend them if they were open to that, but it seems that their heart is set against me. I pray for them, Lord, by name. Reach them. Reach them through me if you will. In the meantime, let my light shine for you in their presence. May I be patient and kind in their midst as I dodge the arrows they send my way.

∽

"If I could hear Christ praying for me in the next room, I would not fear a million enemies. Yet distance makes no difference. He is praying for me."

— Robert Murray McCheyne

My **Energy** Is Divine Energy. I Run on God's Battery

The Truth according to God's Word

He gives strength to the weary
    and increases the power of the weak.
    Even youths grow tired and weary,
    and young men stumble and fall;
    but those who hope in the LORD
    will renew their strength.
    They will soar on wings like eagles;
    they will run and not grow weary,
    they will walk and not be faint. (Isa. 40:29–31)

[Christ] is the one we proclaim, admonishing and teaching everyone with all wisdom, so that we may present everyone fully mature in Christ. To this end I strenuously contend with all the energy Christ so powerfully works in me. (Col. 1:28–29)

The Truth

We are busy people. In all our rushing around, it's easy to become drained of all our emotional and physical energy. But God has a store of energy set aside for us that never runs out. We tap into that energy as we live in the power of his Holy Spirit. What a vast supply! May it keep us going long after our natural strength has ebbed.

Tell Yourself the Truth

"I get tired. I run low on energy. And sometimes when that happens, God calls me to cut back on my activities and rest. Other times, when rest is not an option, God gives me supernatural strength to make it through my day, my week, my month, my year. His Holy Spirit energizes me beyond my own physical powers. Truly he causes me to soar on wings like eagles, to run and not grow weary, to walk and not faint."

Pray the Promise

Heavenly Father, sometimes I'm so busy, I forget to rest. You know my physical needs. Sometimes the need is, indeed, simply to step back and take some time off. Help me recognize those times. And when resting is not the option I can choose, I depend on you to sustain me far beyond what my tired body can muster up. May you give me the energy I need, Lord!

⤺

"Press forward. Do not stop, do not linger in your journey, but strive for the mark set before you."

— GEORGE WHITEFIELD

I Will Live Forever. God's Gift of **Eternal Life** Is Mine

The Truth according to God's Word

Whoever believes in the Son has eternal life, but whoever rejects the Son will not see life, for God's wrath remains on them. (John 3:36)

"Very truly I tell you, whoever hears my word and believes him who sent me has eternal life and will not be judged but has crossed over from death to life." (John 5:24)

For to me, to live is Christ and to die is gain. If I am to go on living in the body, this will mean fruitful labor for me. Yet what shall I choose? I do not know! (Phil. 1:21–22)

And this is what he promised us — eternal life. (1 John 2:25)

The Truth

The gift of eternal life is the gift that can never die. It is, after all, *eternal*. That we who believe in Christ possess this gift is a miracle of all miracles. *Nothing can cause us to die.* When we leave this body, we continue to exist in the presence of God. No wonder Paul didn't know whether to stay here on earth to benefit the believers at Philippi or to go home to heaven. He knew he had eternal life, and he knew heaven was something to be yearned for, not resisted.

Tell Yourself the Truth

"This is what God has promised me: eternal life. I will never die. *Never*. I will live on into eternity, all because of this one precious gift God has given me—and which I possess now—even before I leave this planet. What then can discourage me or cause me to despair over this short span on earth? Nothing! For my real life, my eternal life will not be spent in this aging, aching body. I will live on and on and on in the presence of the one who loves me most—and in a new and perfect body. What a day that will be!"

Pray the Promise

Lord, truly the greatest gift of all is the gift of eternal life. Praise you, Father, that this gift is mine. Thank you that I will never die but will live on far into eternity with you. It truly is the unspeakable gift. And at the cost of Christ on Calvary! I will forever be grateful.

⤳

"If you are born again, eternal life is that quality of life that you possess right now."

—IAN THOMAS

God Can Use Even Me in Evangelism. There Are People Only I Can Reach

The Truth according to God's Word

"Go into all the world and preach the gospel to all creation. Whoever believes and is baptized will be saved, but whoever does not believe will be condemned." (Mark 16:15–16)

And how can anyone preach unless they are sent? As it is written: "How beautiful are the feet of those who bring good news!" (Rom. 10:15)

But you, keep your head in all situations, endure hardship, do the work of an evangelist. (2 Tim. 4:5)

The Truth

Evangelism has been rightly described as one person who was hungry and found bread telling other hungry people about this Man who offers free bread—as much as is desired. Those who are truly hungry will respond, just as we did to this offer of free bread.

Tell Yourself the Truth

"I need have no fear in telling others about Christ. Evangelism can become natural to me as I simply share what has happened to me. I'm not trying to make someone become 'religious.' I'm looking for people who are hungry so that I can tell them about the Bread of Life that satisfies our deepest hunger. God directs such people to me. I am watchful for natural ways to share about this Man who gives free bread. My prayer to be used of God as one who shares the Good News goes before me. This is a prayer God delights to answer, and I will watch for those he brings to me today."

Pray the Promise

Lord, you have given this hungry person bread to eat—Living Bread! Help me be wise about spreading your Good News. I don't want to be a clanging cymbal or say the wrong thing and turn people off. But even more, I do want to see others come to Christ. Give me the words, Lord! Give me the passion to watch for those you bring my way. Help me recognize the opportunities you provide. Lord, I will be a worker in the harvest.

⌒

"Nature teaches us that every believer should be a soul-winner. It is an essential part of the new nature. We see it in every child who loves to tell of his happiness and to bring others to share his joys."

— ANDREW MURRAY

Evil Exists, but God Is Stronger Than Any Evil That Threatens Me

The Truth according to God's Word

Even though I walk
   through the darkest valley,
   I will fear no evil,
   for you are with me;
   your rod and your staff,
   they comfort me. (Ps. 23:4)

"'Deliver us from the evil one.'" (Matt. 6:13)

Hate what is evil; cling to what is good. (Rom. 12:9)

Reject every kind of evil. (1 Thess. 5:22)

The Truth

Evil was not God's original intent. When God created the earth and humankind, he pronounced them "good." But sin entered the world, and thereafter evil took root. Since then, not a human being has lived whose life has not been touched in some way by evil—for some, so much so that they become withdrawn and afraid. But for the Christian, though evil exists and touches our lives, it can do no lasting harm. Greater is he who is in us than he who is in the world.

Tell Yourself the Truth

"Though I live in the midst of evil, I am not a part of its domain. My citizenship is in a kingdom that knows no evil. When evil wants to invade my life, I reject it outright. Nor will I allow evil influences in my home. I stand against evil in society because I know how it traps people who mistakenly think evil is harmless—often to their own destruction. I know that evil is powerful, but not as powerful as Christ in me. For those it has touched and taken captive, I pray to see them rescued, snatched even, from the evil forces holding them prisoner. In my life, I'm determined that good *will* triumph over evil."

Pray the Promise

Lord, you taught me to pray for deliverance from the evil one, and that is my prayer. I despise evil as it encroaches on people I know and love. It even tries to encroach on me. I pray in faith against those influences and invoke, instead, goodness and the presence of Christ to overcome evil. Lord, may you be lifted up in triumph over the forces of evil.

⌒

"If you are under the power of evil and you want to get under the power of God, cry to him to bring you over to his service; cry to him to take you into his army. He will hear you; he will come to you, and, if need be, he will send a legion of angels to help you to fight your way up to heaven. God will take you by the right hand and lead you through this wilderness, over death, and take you right into his kingdom."

— D. L. MOODY

I Strive to Do All Things with **Excellence** for the Lord

The Truth according to God's Word

Finally, brothers and sisters, whatever is true, whatever is noble, whatever is right, whatever is pure, whatever is lovely, whatever is admirable—if anything is excellent or praiseworthy—think about such things. (Phil. 4:8)

Whatever you do, work at it with all your heart, as working for the Lord, not for human masters, since you know that you will receive an inheritance from the Lord as a reward. It is the Lord Christ you are serving. (Col. 3:23–24)

The Truth

When God created the earth, he said it was "very good." But we know that it was more than very good—it was excellent. We, made in his image, are called to excellence in all that we do too. How then can we put forth halfhearted efforts in his service? How can we do less than our best in all we put our hand to? We simply can't. Excellence is the mark of the Christian.

Tell Yourself the Truth

"I am created for excellence, not mediocrity. Everything I put my hand to is an extension of who I am. I do my best for my family, my employer, those I serve, and my God. Anything less than the best is not good enough. I pursue excellence with a passion, in the same way that God does all things with excellence. I train my mind to think positive thoughts of excellence, not negative thoughts of adequacy. The fruit of a life well-lived is the excellence that remains when the life has come to an end."

Pray the Promise

Lord, all your works are excellent! May the same be said of my works.

◡

"The secret of living a life of excellence is merely a matter of thinking thoughts of excellence. Really, it's a matter of programming our minds with the kind of information that will set us free."

— CHUCK SWINDOLL

I Will Set No Wicked Thing before My Eyes

The Truth according to God's Word

I will set nothing wicked before my eyes. (Ps. 101:3 NKJV)

My son, give me your heart
and let your eyes delight in my ways. (Prov. 23:26)

"Your eye is the lamp of your body. When your eyes are healthy, your whole body also is full of light. But when they are unhealthy, your body also is full of darkness." (Luke 11:34)

The Truth

Our eyes are a point of entry into our brains. What we see affects us greatly. No wonder Jesus said that if our eyes offend us, we are to pluck them out. But rather than plucking them out, why not train them to see good, not evil? We can and must be careful what we rest our eyes on. Unguarded eyes have been the downfall of many a Christian.

Tell Yourself the Truth

"My eyes are the lamp of my body. What I take in through my eyes will be digested by my inner man. Every image is projected on the movie screen of my mind. For that reason, I guard my eyes from evil. Like David, *I will set nothing wicked before my eyes.*"

Pray the Promise

Lord, I will set nothing wicked before my eyes. Sometimes this is hard, Father, because inappropriate images abound in my world. Set a guard, therefore, before me, Lord. Let my eyes not stray, but let their gaze bounce off of images that portray sin as good. Give me eyes to see as you see, Lord—pure eyes.

෧

O be careful little eyes what you see.
O be careful little eyes what you see.
There's a Father up above,
And he's looking down in love,
So be careful little eyes what you see.

— CHILDREN'S SUNDAY SCHOOL SONG

My Past **Failures** Can Become Stepping-Stones to My Success

The Truth according to God's Word

Create in me a pure heart, O God,
and renew a steadfast spirit within me.
Do not cast me from your presence
or take your Holy Spirit from me.
Restore to me the joy of your salvation
and grant me a willing spirit, to sustain me. (Ps. 51:10–12)

Brothers and sisters, I do not consider myself yet to have taken hold of it. But one thing I do: Forgetting what is behind and straining toward what is ahead, I press on toward the goal to win the prize for which God has called me heavenward in Christ Jesus. (Phil. 3:13–14)

The Truth

God doesn't keep track of our successes and failures. Aren't you glad? Sometimes our so-called failures are merely disappointed expectations that serve the good lesson of showing us our own inabilities. Peter knew that. His three denials of Christ were later followed by Jesus restoring him as he instructed Peter three times, "Feed my sheep." The apostle Paul knew that his own past was rubbish and best forgotten as he pressed on for what God had next for him.

The truth is we may never find our own "next" if we keep reliving the past. Instead, let's let our past—no matter how many failures we've had—remain in our past.

Look up. Look ahead. God is in your future, so rejoice. Again I say rejoice!

Tell Yourself the Truth

"I can't count the number of times I've failed. But so what? God isn't counting, so neither should I. Failure is only about the past, and God has forgotten the sins, mistakes, and failures of my past. My eyes are set on the future and the successes that God will bring my way. Failure has no place in my present or future."

Pray the Promise

You've seen how miserably I've failed, Lord. And yet you never bring it up. I know that's because you've chosen to forget the sins and failures in my past. Help me also, Father, to set them aside forever. Help me to see how dead and gone my past is so that I can concentrate on my future.

⇛

"Don't waste time and fritter away faith by ... mourning over the failures of yesterday and the long ago. Commit them to God and look upward and onward."

— SAMUEL LOGAN BRENGLE

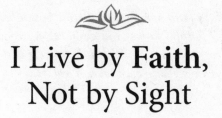

I Live by **Faith**, Not by Sight

The Truth according to God's Word

I have chosen the way of faithfulness. (Ps. 119:30)

We live by faith, not by sight. (2 Cor. 5:7 – 8)

This is the victory that has overcome the world, even our faith. (1 John 5:4)

The Truth

Faith is easy. So easy that a child can have the kind of faith God rewards. But as grown-ups, we complicate faith. Let's just believe all that God tells us about him and about us. Such simple faith changes everything.

Tell Yourself the Truth

"I am a child of God through faith. I overcome the world through my faith. I overcome doubts, sin, worry, and every possible trial by simple childlike faith. I nourish my faith by knowing God's Word and applying it to my life. Faith is the blazing torch by which I walk fearlessly into the future God has for me."

Pray the Promise

Father, I walk by faith, not by sight. I trust in you because you have proved yourself faithful to me. You do miracles in my life and take me places I never dreamed of. What is impossible with me is possible with you. Increase my faith even more, Lord.

❧

"Faith doesn't operate in the realm of the possible. There is no glory for God in that which man can do. Faith begins where man's power ends."

— GEORGE MUELLER

God Cares about My Family

The Truth according to God's Word

For I will pour water on the thirsty land,
  and streams on the dry ground;
  I will pour out my Spirit on your offspring,
  and my blessing on your descendants. (Isa. 44:3)

He will bring you a message through which you and all your household will be saved. (Acts 11:14)

"Believe in the Lord Jesus, and you will be saved — you and your household." (Acts 16:31)

The Truth

Sometimes when we make spiritual progress, we look back and see that our families are not following us. They're stuck where they have been for years, or worse, they seem to be going in the wrong direction. When we experience Christ for ourselves, we naturally want our families to find what we've found. And in the Bible, we see that very thing happen time after time as in both the Old Testament and the New Testament entire households followed God.

Such a miracle as "household salvation" has to be of God. Because no matter how much we tell our family members about Christ, they often are the hardest people to reach. But that's not a reason to give up. We must keep on praying and believing for our households.

Tell Yourself the Truth

"I pray in faith for my family to love and serve God, and to that end I will live a Christ-honoring life before them. I believe my family *will* be saved. God has heard my prayers and will do what it takes to bring them to himself. Throughout the Bible, God was faithful to save entire households. Noah's family was saved; Rahab's too. Among the Hebrews, each family was saved by the sacrifice of the Passover lamb; the household of Zacchaeus was saved, as well as the households of Cornelius, Lydia, the Philippian jailer, Crispus, Stephanas, and others. I am therefore believing God to save my entire household too."

Pray the Promise

God, in your Word, I see you saving entire families time after time. I'm claiming my own household and asking that you bring salvation to all within my family circle. Open hearts, God, that I can't seem to reach. Help me live your truth and your love in front of them. Yes, miracles, Lord. That's what it will take. Save my family, Lord; this I pray.

⌒

"A man ought to live so that everybody knows he is a Christian ... and most of all, his family ought to know."

— D. L. MOODY

I Have **Favor** from Other People

The Truth according to God's Word

And the boy Samuel continued to grow in stature and in favor with the LORD and with people. (1 Sam. 2:26)

Surely, LORD, you bless the righteous;
    you surround them with your favor as with a shield. (Ps. 5:12)

May the favor of the Lord our God rest on us;
    establish the work of our hands for us —
    yes, establish the work of our hands. (Ps. 90:17)

But he gives us more grace. That is why Scripture says: "God opposes the proud but shows favor to the humble." (James 4:6)

The Truth

The Bible is full of stories of God's favor on his people — and promises of favor for us, too. Yes, God still grants favor to his children. Expect it in your life.

Tell Yourself the Truth

"The favor of the Lord rests on me. This is not something I can buy or bargain for God to give me. It's purely one of his gifts to his children. Favor precedes me when I enter into negotiations. Favor finds a way for me to prevail with my enemies. Favor moves me more quickly along God's path for me. Favor moves quietly though. It is not loud or boastful about its presence. Daily I walk in the knowledge of God's favor preceding me in all I do."

Pray the Promise

Father of lights, thank you for the great favor you've given me—favor both from you and from other people. May you continue to surround me with your favor as with a shield. I pray, as did your servant Moses, that the favor of the Lord would rest on me. May your favor on my life result in honor and praise to you and the completion of your will in my life.

↬

"If thou wouldst find much favor and peace with God and man, be very low in thine own eyes."

— ROBERT LEIGHTON

I **Fear** Nothing

The Truth according to God's Word

The LORD is the strength of my life;
  Of whom shall I be afraid? (Ps. 27:1 NKJV)

Fear not [there is nothing to fear], for I am with you; do not look
around you in terror and be dismayed, for I am your God. I will
strengthen and harden you to difficulties, yes, I will help you; yes,
I will hold you up and retain you with My [victorious] right hand
of rightness and justice. (Isa. 41:10 AMP)

"The very hairs of your head are all numbered. Don't be afraid;
you are worth more than many sparrows." (Luke 12:7)

The Truth

We may be surprised to find out that Jesus' number one command was "Fear not!" Not just Jesus, but over and over in the
Bible, God instructs us to "fear not." And why should we never be
fearful? Because he is always with us to strengthen us, to encourage us in difficulties, and to help and protect us. His love carries
with it a power far stronger than any object of our fear. We are of
great value to God. We need never fear. *Never.*

Tell Yourself the Truth

"I will not be ruled by fear. I stand boldly before that which tempts me to fear, and render it powerless over my emotions. The Lord himself is my Protector; I need no other. He causes me not to fear as I draw strength after strength after strength from him. To the natural eye, there may be reasons for me to fear, but I don't rely on natural eyes. I see through eyes of faith that are focused on Jesus. He empowers me to slay the fearful giants that come against me. In Christ, I'm resilient, immovable, immune to the fear that would destroy me."

Pray the Promise

Lord, I rejoice in the victory over my fears! I praise you for the boldness I can have in the face of fear. I take strength in knowing that you guard me from the fear of evil and danger. No matter what tactics Satan uses, I will fear no evil because of you.

⌇

"Only he who can say, 'The Lord is the strength of my life,' can say, 'Of whom shall I be afraid?' "

— ALEXANDER MACLAREN

The **Fear of God** Is the Beginning of Wisdom

The Truth according to God's Word

The fear of the LORD is the beginning of wisdom,
  and knowledge of the Holy One is understanding. (Prov. 9:10)

He will be the sure foundation for your times,
  a rich store of salvation and wisdom and knowledge;
  the fear of the LORD is the key to this treasure. (Isa. 33:6)

Show proper respect to everyone, love the family of believers, fear God, honor the emperor. (1 Peter 2:17)

The Truth

We sometimes are so taken with the love of God that we forget there is also an awesomeness and holiness about God that is to be feared. Nothing has changed since Isaiah wrote that the fear of God is the key to the rich store of salvation, wisdom, and knowledge. Yes, it is good and right to fear God.

Tell Yourself the Truth

"The fear of the Lord is pure, enduring forever. The fear of God is the beginning of wisdom for me. I live daily in the wonderful,

POWER IN THE PROMISES

cleansing, awesome fear of the Lord. I see in God a majesty that compels me to fear him in the healthy way that brings about the needed changes in my life. To know the fear of God is to know in a small measure my need for holiness. I revel in the fear of my great God. It releases me from all other fears."

Pray the Promise

Father, I fall on my knees in praise to you for your greatness. Yes, I do fear you, but this fear is clean and pure, enduring forever. You are greatly to be praised—and greatly to be feared.

༄

"The remarkable thing about God is that when you fear God, you fear nothing else, whereas if you do not fear God, you fear everything else."

— OSWALD CHAMBERS

Food Is to Nourish My Body. I Will Eat Responsibly

The Truth according to God's Word

All creatures look to you
to give them their food at the proper time. (Ps. 104:27)

He provides food for those who fear him;
he remembers his covenant forever. (Ps. 111:5)

" 'Give us today our daily bread.' " (Matt. 6:11)

"Therefore I tell you, do not worry about your life, what you will eat or drink; or about your body, what you will wear. Is not life more than food, and the body more than clothes?" (Matt. 6:25)

The Truth

Food, like so many other things, can become an addiction. Either we eat too much or we starve ourselves—and either can be an eating disorder. Often this happens because of the way we see ourselves—almost always wrongly. We see our body as imperfect and want to change it. Another cause can be our quest to self-medicate our pain with food. Thus the popular term "comfort food."

The answer for our negative self-image and our pain is not found in the consumption of food. The answer lies in attaining the right perception of ourselves, including our bodies. When we can accept ourselves as the beloved of God, we can accept much about ourselves that is indeed imperfect. We can overcome our pain through trusting God's promises, not by using food to self-medicate.

Abandon your quest for the perfect body. Abandon your pain by receiving healing from God. Then eat with gratitude what God provides. Enjoy your daily food, but make it your practice to neither overeat nor undereat.

Tell Yourself the Truth

"I accept the body God gave me. I will take good care of my body in order to honor God with my health and to love him with all my strength, not because I want to conform to the way society says I should look. Food is not an idol to me; it's how I keep my body functioning properly. I will not allow myself to be subject to cravings for foods that are not good for me. I eat what God provides. I will not overindulge or underindulge but will entrust my body and my weight to God as I eat properly and exercise daily. God will be glorified in my body."

Pray the Promise

Father, you are my provider of all things. With thankfulness I eat the food you provide. I'm also thankful for the healthy body you've given me. I will not overfeed it, nor will I starve it. Lord, be glorified in my body.

"Numerous Christians do not know how to glorify God in their eating and drinking. They do not eat and drink simply to keep their body fit for the Lord's use but indulge to satisfy their personal desires. We should understand that the body is for the Lord and not for ourselves; hence we should refrain from using it for our pleasure. Food ought not hinder our fellowship with God since it is to be taken purely to preserve the body in health."

— WATCHMAN NEE

I Fully **Forgive** Those Who Have Sinned against Me

The Truth according to God's Word

" 'And forgive us our debts,
    as we also have forgiven our debtors.
    And lead us not into temptation,
    but deliver us from the evil one.'
"For if you forgive other people when they sin against you, your heavenly Father will also forgive you. But if you do not forgive others their sins, your Father will not forgive your sins." (Matt. 6:12–15)

"If your brother or sister sins against you, rebuke them; and if they repent, forgive them. Even if they sin against you seven times in a day and seven times come back to you saying 'I repent,' you must forgive them." (Luke 17:3–4)

Bear with each other and forgive one another if any of you has a grievance against someone. Forgive as the Lord forgave you. (Col. 3:13)

The Truth

Complete forgiveness is what the Christian life is about. God has forgiven us of much, and so we are enabled to forgive the sins others have committed against us. Though this is often hard to do, it's much easier when we fully grasp the magnitude of our own sins and the immense and gracious forgiveness God has extended to us. It's also easier when we consider the damage to our own souls when we don't forgive.

Tell Yourself the Truth

"Because I'm a forgiven person, I am also a forgiving person. I release those who have sinned against me from any guilt or bitterness I've held against them. In setting them free, I'm setting myself free. By faith, forgiveness is a way of life for me. No one can offend me to the point of unforgiveness. All is forgiven — from God to me and from me to all others."

Pray the Promise

Because you forgive me, Lord, it's not so very hard for me to release those who have sinned against me. In your name, Father, I do now release every person I've been harboring bitterness and unforgiveness against. I ask you now to bring great blessing into their lives. May they and I move on from the sins of the past.

∽

"To be a Christian means to forgive the inexcusable, because God has forgiven the inexcusable in you."

— C. S. LEWIS

God Has a Successful **Future** for Me

The Truth according to God's Word

Consider the blameless, observe the upright;
   a future awaits those who seek peace. (Ps. 37:37)

There is surely a future hope for you,
   and your hope will not be cut off. (Prov. 23:18)

"For I know the plans I have for you," declares the LORD, "plans to prosper you and not to harm you, plans to give you hope and a future." (Jer. 29:11)

The Truth

Too often we fall prey to worrying about the future. We think "what if" so-and-so happens? What if we get sick, lose our spouse, lose our job, lose a child, lose our money, and more? There's no end to the things we can worry about in our future. But there's a solution to that worry. By an act of faith, we can surrender our future entirely to God. A future left in God's hands allows us to walk in complete confidence in the years ahead. After all, God *does* plan to bring blessing, not cursing, to our future. Trust him for your future and be set free from the "what-ifs" of life.

Tell Yourself the Truth

"I have a good future ahead of me because I have given that future over to God. He directs my path. He opens future doors and closes past doors. God will bring great blessing to my life; therefore I don't worry about what may happen. I immediately silence the negative voices that whisper that my future is bleak. Instead, I pray in faith and walk expectantly into a future where God has already been. Each morning I open the gift that is my future."

Pray the Promise

What a blessed future you have for me, Father! I believe it because I know you love me and have asked me to trust you in all things, even those things I can't see with my natural eyes, but which are clearly visible through the eyes of faith.

Lord, you are there in my future already. Each of my tomorrows has your handprint on it; therefore I don't worry about what tomorrow may bring.

～

"God is down in front. He is in the tomorrows. It is tomorrow that fills men with dread. God is there already. All the tomorrows of our life have to pass him before they can get to us."

— F. B. MEYER

Because God Is **Generous** to Me, I Too Am Generous

The Truth according to God's Word

Give generously ... and do so without a grudging heart; then because of this the LORD your God will bless you in all your work and in everything you put your hand to. (Deut. 15:10)

Good will come to those who are generous and lend freely,
    who conduct their affairs with justice. (Ps. 112:5)

A generous person will prosper;
    whoever refreshes others will be refreshed. (Prov. 11:25)

"Remember the words of the Lord Jesus, that He said, 'It is more blessed to give than to receive.'" (Acts 20:35 NKJV)

Command them to do good, to be rich in good deeds, and to be generous and willing to share. (1 Tim. 6:18)

The Truth

If you want to be blessed "in everything you put your hand to," have a generous spirit. *Give.* Not out of compulsion, but out of the largeness of your heart. God sets the example for us in being a giving, generous Father to us. Not only are we not to give grudgingly, but we're to give our best, our "firstfruits." Make it your practice to give to God's work from the first of your income; don't wait and see what's left over at the end. Put God and others before yourself and be blessed. Giving is a bigger blessing than receiving.

Tell Yourself the Truth

"My income is dependent on God, not my job, the government, or my savings, so I can be a generous person. God has made me a steward over all that comes my way. I do not hold tight to my purse strings when it comes to giving to the people and the causes God directs me to. I'm not foolish with my money, but prudent, so that what I do give goes further and accomplishes the work God intends. I'm a channel through which God can bring resources to me to give to others and to meet my needs."

Pray the Promise

Thank you, God, for treating me so generously. As you give to me, so do I give to others, gladly and without regrets. Because of your example, I'm generous in small things, such as tipping for good service, and generous in larger things, such as giving to ministries that spread your Word. I also give to those in need and try to do so anonymously so that you are given the credit rather than me. Thank you for your kindness toward me, Father.

⌒

"Do not think me mad. It is not to make money that I believe a Christian should live. The noblest thing a man can do is, just humbly to receive, and then go amongst others and give."

— DAVID LIVINGSTONE

There Are No Barriers between Me and God's Love

The Truth according to God's Word

How priceless is your unfailing love, O God! (Ps. 36:7)

Give thanks to the God of heaven.
His love endures forever. (Ps. 136:26)

"For God so loved the world that he gave his one and only Son, that whoever believes in him shall not perish but have eternal life." (John 3:16)

I am convinced that neither death nor life, neither angels nor demons, neither the present nor the future, nor any powers, neither height nor depth, nor anything else in all creation, will be able to separate us from the love of God that is in Christ Jesus our Lord. (Rom. 8:38–39)

See what great love the Father has lavished on us, that we should be called children of God! (1 John 3:1)

God is love. (1 John 4:8)

The Truth

Did you know that God loves each of us as much as he loves his Son? He gave his Son *for* us. What does that say about the depth of your Father's love for you? And did you know there is *nothing* that can separate you from this love? Satan can't do it. Your boss can't do it. Your family can't do it. Your government can't do it. Even *you* can't do it. When you came to Christ, the one thing that separated you from God—your sin—was forever taken away on the cross. Now there is no barrier—there *can* be no barrier to the all-consuming love God has for you. *Live* in that love. Make it your home. Keep God's love at the forefront of your mind. Overflow with God's love toward others. Never, never believe you are separated from God's love.

Tell Yourself the Truth

"I am loved by God in ways I can never comprehend. His love for me is always present, always enduring. Nothing in this universe has the power to stop God's love for me. God's love keeps me for himself; it cleanses me and it motivates me to love others. God's love is the sustaining force of my life. I know there is no barrier to keep God's love from reaching me. No such thing exists."

Pray the Promise

God, truly your love is enough! Sufficient love to heal all my wounds and to keep me satisfied, happy, and looking forward to the culmination of that love when I stand before you. Oh, if only we could all have a glimpse of that love—our lives would be forever changed! The world would be forever changed. What love!

~

"Nothing can separate you from God's love, absolutely nothing.
God is enough for time; God is enough for eternity. God is enough!"

— HANNAH WHITALL SMITH

Jesus Is Lord during the Good Times Too

The Truth according to God's Word

This is the day the LORD has made;
  We will rejoice and be glad in it. (Ps. 118:24 NKJV)

Give thanks in all circumstances; for this is God's will for you in Christ Jesus. (1 Thess. 5:18)

The Truth

So often we call on God during hard times, and that's to be expected. But what about the good times? How do we think God reacts to our good times? I suspect he would be delighted to hear our prayers and praises then too. In truth, our words of gratitude and petition to God are just as important when things are going right. God is our ever-present God in all of our times — good and bad. We must praise him during both.

Tell Yourself the Truth

"My life has its good seasons and its hard seasons. I'm aware of God's closeness during both. Just as I know he feels my pain during trials, I trust that he also feels my joy during the good times.

I glorify God daily regardless of the circumstances, and it makes a difference."

Pray the Promise

Father, I'll admit I love the good times in my life, but the bad times—not so much. But for all you bring into my life, I am grateful, for this is your express will—that in all things I should give thanks. Thanks be to you, then. In good times and bad. Now and always.

～

"Thou who has given so much to me, give one thing more: a grateful heart."

— GEORGE HERBERT

God's **Grace** Is Greater Than My Sin

The Truth according to God's Word

In him we have redemption through his blood, the forgiveness of sins, in accordance with the riches of God's grace. (Eph. 1:7)

He has saved us and called us to a holy life—not because of anything we have done but because of his own purpose and grace. This grace was given us in Christ Jesus before the beginning of time, but it has now been revealed through the appearing of our Savior, Christ Jesus, who has destroyed death and has brought life and immortality to light through the gospel. (2 Tim. 1:9–10)

Be strong in the grace that is in Christ Jesus. (2 Tim. 2:1)

The Truth

Grace came through Jesus Christ. *Grace*. As someone has wisely noted, grace is "**G**od's **R**iches **A**t **C**hrist's **E**xpense." We receive grace because Christ paid the penalty for our sins. We sometimes hear people talk about "cheap grace" that enables us to be careless about sin, but the person who fully grasps God's grace finds sin repellant. We must never think that grace means the license to do what we want or that there was no cost paid for our grace. The most expensive purchase ever made in the entire universe was the price of grace.

Tell Yourself the Truth

"I don't take the grace of God lightly. To me, grace was never cheap. A high price was paid so that I might live under grace, not law. I will live *strong* in the grace that is in Christ Jesus. I will never cheapen grace by sinning willfully, nor will I cheapen it by turning back to the law as a means of pleasing God."

Pray the Promise

Father, thank you for grace! It is my only hope of salvation—and it is mine! Grace, wondrous grace.

∾

"It is grace at the beginning, and grace at the end. So that when you and I come to lie upon our death beds, the one thing that should comfort and help and strengthen us there is the thing that helped us in the beginning. Not what we have been, not what we have done, but the grace of God in Jesus Christ our Lord. The Christian life starts with grace, it must continue with grace, it ends with grace. Grace wondrous grace."

— Martyn Lloyd Jones

I Am No Longer **Guilty** — God Forgave All My Sins

The Truth according to God's Word

Then I acknowledged my sin to you
    and did not cover up my iniquity.
    I said, "I will confess
    my transgressions to the LORD."
And you forgave
    the guilt of my sin. (Ps. 32:5)

Let us draw near to God with a sincere heart and with the full assurance that faith brings, having our hearts sprinkled to cleanse us from a guilty conscience and having our bodies washed with pure water. (Heb. 10:22)

The Truth

Guilt is real. It's real because transgressions are real. But, praise God, he has a solution for our transgressions and our guilt: the atoning sacrifice of Christ. So while guilt is real, the solution to guilt is even more real: confess, repent, and walk in God's forgiveness. That's the only solution, and it's enough.

Tell Yourself the Truth

"I thank God that I need never be burdened by guilt again. Though it was my sin that brought about my guilt, God has dealt a death blow to my sin at the cross. Yes, Christ took my sins and my guilt along with it. Why then should I continue to carry that which no longer exists in God's mind? The truth is, I shouldn't. I should walk free, like a prisoner on death row who, as he's walking to the execution chamber is, instead, escorted to the prison door and released into the outside world—a free man because someone else took that long walk in his place. I thank God for sending Christ to take my place—and to take my guilt."

Pray the Promise

My guilt is gone, Lord. Forever gone. Thank you for the exchange you made on the cross: an innocent sacrifice in the person of Christ in the place of me and my rightful guilty verdict. Thank you that I walk free in you every day.

～

"When a man has judged himself, Satan is put out of office. When he lays anything to a saint's charge, he is able to retort and say, 'It is true, Satan, I am guilty of these sins, but I have judged myself already for them; and having condemned myself in the lower court of conscience, God will acquit me in the upper court of heaven.'"

— THOMAS WATSON

Happiness Comes from Knowing Christ

The Truth according to God's Word

May the righteous be glad
  and rejoice before God;
    may they be happy and joyful. (Ps. 68:3)

Happy are the people whose God is the LORD! (Ps. 144:15 NKJV)

Is anyone among you in trouble? Let them pray. Is anyone happy?
Let them sing songs of praise. (James 5:13)

The Truth

Happiness is the natural state of the Christian—it is a by-product
of living a Christ-centered life. If we want to be happy, we'll do
the things that make for happiness and avoid the things that make
for unhappiness. It just so happens, however, that many times
we're attracted to the things (and people) that make for unhappiness. Learning to be happy means reorienting ourselves to Christ
as the center of our lives and to God's greater purposes.

Tell Yourself the Truth

"To seek happiness, I must first seek Christ himself, for he is the source of all true happiness. I know by experience the things that rob me of happiness and I eliminate them one by one from my life. The years are too short to be burdened down with the weight of unhappiness. Daily I will make it my early business to make my soul happy in the Lord."

Pray the Promise

Today I take happiness as my lot, Lord. I turn away from the sadnesses that tempt me to despair, and I look to you, to Christ, as my sufficiency. Great is my happiness, Lord, because I am yours and you are mine.

෴

"More than forty years [ago] I saw ... that the first great and primary business to which I ought to attend every day was to have my soul happy in the Lord."

— GEORGE MUELLER

Hard Times Come, but God Keeps Me Strong through Them

The Truth according to God's Word

God is our refuge and strength,
    an ever-present help in trouble. (Ps. 46:1)

"Call on me in the day of trouble;
    I will deliver you, and you will honor me." (Ps. 50:15)

Then they cried to the LORD in their trouble,
    and he saved them from their distress.
    He sent out his word and healed them;
    he rescued them from the grave. (Ps. 107:19–20)

The Truth

Everyone must pass through the fire of hard times. No one is exempt. What matters is how we react during those times. Are we steadfastly looking at Jesus as we walk on the stormy waves, or do we look at the water beneath our feet and become fearful? Reacting in faith during hard times brings us through with far less wear and tear on our souls.

Tell Yourself the Truth

"I've endured hard times before, and I will endure them again. When they come, I hide in my God, my Deliverer, while he brings me through to better times again. Storms are for only a season. Sunshine eventually follows. Until then I stay strong and hear Jesus say, 'It's all right. I'm here to walk through this with you.'"

Pray the Promise

Hard times are here again, Lord. I look back to the storms we've weathered together in the past, and I know we'll weather this one too. But each time, it still seems so hard. Help me, Father, as I fix my gaze on Jesus, my companion through this rough patch. Stay close, Lord, closer than ever. We will surely rejoice together on the other side of this hard time.

∽

"No matter what storm you face, you need to know that God loves you. He has not abandoned you."

— FRANKLIN GRAHAM

God Supplies My Good Health Day by Day

The Truth according to God's Word

Praise the LORD, my soul,
and forget not all his benefits —
who forgives all your sins
and heals all your diseases,
who redeems your life from the pit
and crowns you with love and compassion. (Ps. 103:2 – 4)

Do not be wise in your own eyes;
fear the LORD and shun evil.
This will bring health to your body
and nourishment to your bones. (Prov. 3:7 – 8)

My son, pay attention to what I say;
turn your ear to my words.
Do not let them out of your sight,
keep them within your heart;
for they are life to those who find them
and health to one's whole body. (Prov. 4:20 – 22)

Is anyone among you sick? Let them call the elders of the church to pray over them and anoint them with oil in the name of the Lord. And the prayer offered in faith will make the sick person well; the Lord will raise them up. If they have sinned, they will be forgiven. (James 5:14–15)

I pray that you may enjoy good health and that all may go well with you, even as your soul is getting along well. (3 John 1:2)

The Truth

No one likes to be sick. Ask chronically ill persons if they want to be well and they are sure to shout, "Yes!" But in the midst of illness, it's hard to see ourselves coming out well on the other side. We think, *What if I don't get better? What if I suffer? What if my family is inconvenienced? What if this causes financial hardship? What if I die?*

God doesn't want us to think about the what-ifs. He wants us to come out of this disease in health or in heaven. It's often easy just to give in when we're sick and let nature take its course. It's harder to envision ourselves back at work fulfilling God's plan for us. But that should be our hope, and we should pray to that end.

God is the fountain of good health—whether he's keeping us in good health or restoring us to good health when we're sick. Sometimes he restores us in an instant as he divinely heals us. Other times he restores our health more slowly. Sometimes he uses doctors. Sometimes natural means. But in every case, God is there, brooding over us, caring for us, nursing us as a mother would.

In the meantime as we pray, we should also heed a good doctor's advice, take measures to restore our health by changing any bad habits we might have, and press forward to recovery. God works best with those whose focus is on the future, not the present.

Tell Yourself the Truth

"God owns me—body, soul, and spirit. I trust him to keep all three parts of my being in good health. When symptoms of illness or weakness appear, I take measures to restore my health, pray, and trust God for the results. I am confident in God as my source of health and praise him daily for taking care of my body. When I'm sick, God is not absent. He's here, and he can heal me. He is the ultimate physician and the restorer of my health. I will emerge from this sickness a stronger, happier person, or I will be gathered into his presence. If I have more work to do on this earth, God will restore me to good health. To that end, I cooperate with him by doing the things that make for health, and I will count on him to bring me back to full health. I will eat good food, exercise, rest, and commit my way to him. God will restore my health both through natural means and his healing touch. May my health be a testimony to God's ability to restore the broken and bring them to health."

Pray the Promise

Good health comes from you, O Lord. I rely on you as my chief physician, nutritionist, therapist, and adviser. Show me exactly what I need to do to enjoy good health. I know that hearing and obeying your Word is a source of life. Therefore staying in the Bible is important to my health. Speak to me from your Word, Lord; I'm listening.

⌇

"Christian, who art sick, if thou wilt really seek to know what is the will of God in this thing, do not let thyself be influenced by the opinions of others, nor by thy own former prejudices, but listen to and study what the Word of God has to say. Examine whether it does not tell thee that divine healing is a part of the redemption of Jesus, and that God wills that every believer should have the right to claim it; see whether it does not promise that the prayer of every child of God for this thing shall be heard, and whether health restored by the power of the Holy Spirit does not manifest the glory of God in the eyes of the church and of the world."

— ANDREW MURRAY

I Am Already a Citizen of Heaven. Someday It Will Be My Permanent Home

The Truth according to God's Word

"My Father's house has many rooms; if that were not so, would I have told you that I am going there to prepare a place for you? And if I go and prepare a place for you, I will come back and take you to be with me that you also may be where I am. You know the way to the place where I am going." (John 14:2–4)

"What no eye has seen,
    What no ear has heard,
    and what no human mind has conceived"
    the things God has prepared for those who love him —
these are the things God has revealed to us by his Spirit. (1 Cor. 2:9–10)

Our citizenship is in heaven. And we eagerly await a Savior from there, the Lord Jesus Christ, who, by the power that enables him to bring everything under his control, will transform our lowly bodies so that they will be like his glorious body. (Phil. 3:20–21)

"He will wipe every tear from their eyes. There will be no more death or mourning or crying or pain, for the old order of things has passed away." He who was seated on the throne said, "I am making everything new!" (Rev. 21:4–5)

The Truth

God has prepared a place for us — a *home*. Christians, in fact, often use the word *homesick* to describe our longing for heaven. Though our lives here on earth may be long or short, we know that our lives in heaven will be eternal. Oh how we yearn for that life when we will actually *see* God!

Tell Yourself the Truth

"Heaven is glorious! Earthly words can't describe what my home in heaven will look like. But by faith, I see it and I long to be caught up in an eternity that knows nothing of sadness, sickness, or sin — only pure joy and belonging. I'm so ready!"

Pray the Promise

Father, this life is but a preparation for heaven. With my eyes on eternity, I walk ahead day by day toward that glorious and final destination, eager for my true home with you.

〜

"We talk about heaven being so far away. It is within speaking distance to those who belong there. Heaven is a prepared place for a prepared people."

— D. L. MOODY

The **Holy Spirit** Lives in Me and Guides, Comforts, and Instructs Me

The Truth according to God's Word

"If you then, though you are evil, know how to give good gifts to your children, how much more will your Father in heaven give the Holy Spirit to those who ask him!" (Luke 11:13)

"But the Advocate, the Holy Spirit, whom the Father will send in my name, will teach you all things and will remind you of everything I have said to you." (John 14:26)

May the God of hope fill you with all joy and peace as you trust in him, so that you may overflow with hope by the power of the Holy Spirit. (Rom. 15:13)

When you believed, you were marked in him with a seal, the promised Holy Spirit, who is a deposit guaranteeing our inheritance until the redemption of those who are God's possession— to the praise of his glory. (Eph. 1:13–14)

The Truth

Every believer was created to be a container—a vessel. Our content is the Holy Spirit of God. The apostle Paul says the Holy

Spirit is a down payment for heaven. He says we are sealed by the Spirit—the one who is called our Guide, Comforter, and Instructor—until the day of our redemption. A person who is empowered daily by the Holy Spirit residing within is truly experiencing *life*.

Tell Yourself the Truth

"God lives in me in the person of the Holy Spirit. It is his life that people see in my life. He gives me wisdom beyond myself; he leads me to divine appointments; and he gives me gifts to minister to others. He comforts me, counsels me, cautions me, leads me, and causes me to 'overflow with hope' by his power. I will yield to God's Holy Spirit in all I do."

Pray the Promise

Lord, perhaps the most wonderful aspect of life in you is that you do not work on us from the outside, but you actually come to dwell in your people in the person of the Holy Spirit. You live in us. We are the temple of your Spirit. It's just so unfathomable—yet true! Lord, keep me aware each day that I'm not walking this walk in my own strength, but you are walking this walk through me. You are the hand inside the glove of my life leading me where I should go. Praise you, Father, for your wonderful Holy Spirit!

﹏

"Take this as the secret of Christ's life in you: his Spirit dwells in your innermost spirit. Meditate on it, believe in it, and remember it until this glorious truth produces within you a holy fear and wonderment that the Holy Spirit indeed abides in you!"

— WATCHMAN NEE

I Set Aside All Forms of **Idolatry** in My Life

The Truth according to God's Word

Therefore, my dear friends, flee from idolatry. (1 Cor. 10:14)

For of this you can be sure: No immoral, impure or greedy person—such a person is an idolater—has any inheritance in the kingdom of Christ and of God. (Eph. 5:5)

Put to death, therefore, whatever belongs to your earthly nature: sexual immorality, impurity, lust, evil desires and greed, which is idolatry. (Col. 3:5)

Dear children, keep yourselves from idols. (1 John 5:21)

The Truth

Sometimes we associate idolatry with ancient pagan cultures. But idolatry exists all around us. An idol is anything we put before God. An idol can be money, position, fame, sex, drugs, alcohol, a person we love, or even, yes, a man-made idol created to be worshiped as in the aforementioned pagan cultures. Some people do indeed still pray to idols made with human hands. Others simply give their allegiance to pleasure or materialism, which is also idolatrous.

Tell Yourself the Truth

"Idols are a snare. They lead those who worship them away from the right path. I understand that anything I put before my relationship with God is an idol, and I remove all idols from any place they hold in my life and my heart. Further, I repent of any idols I've worshiped—whether mental idols or physical idols—and turn my worship to God alone."

Pray the Promise

Lord, down through the centuries you have kindly delivered those who love you from their idols. I ask that you reveal to me anything in my life that I've put before you. I want you to be my first priority—and idols of any kind are to have no priority in my life.

❧

"As long as you want anything very much, especially more than you want God, it is an idol."

— A. B. SIMPSON

With God Nothing Is Impossible

The Truth according to God's Word

"Is anything too hard for the LORD?" (Gen. 18:14)

"I am the LORD, the God of all mankind. Is anything too hard for me?" (Jer. 32:27)

"If you have faith as small as a mustard seed, you can say to this mountain, 'Move from here to there' and it will move." (Matt. 17:20)

"Everything is possible for one who believes." (Mark 9:23)

"What is impossible with man is possible with God." (Luke 18:27)

The Truth

Sometimes life rolls along smoothly, and then we hit a mountain named Impossible. Impossible to climb over, go around, go under, go through. We see no way to go ahead. In reality, that's a truly great place to be. Why? Because that's when we really are forced to give God room to work. When our own abilities can solve the problem, we tend to rely less on God. But when Mount Impossible looms before us, what more can we do? And that's when God can work best. For with God, nothing is impossible. What is *your* Mount Impossible? If you have only mustard-seed-sized faith, God can remove that mountain by his power and in his timing.

Tell Yourself the Truth

"Once in a while I have a situation in my life that can only be called 'impossible.' I can only take my hands off the situation and turn it over to the One for whom *nothing* is impossible. I give God room. What else can I do? *Nothing....* Except praise God for his mighty power."

Pray the Promise

Lord, what am I to do? There is no human way through this mountain in front of me. I'm giving you all the room you need. Please remove it from my path. If you don't, nothing will happen. Plow through, Lord. Plow through!

∽

"There are three stages in the work of God: Impossible; Difficult; Done."

— HUDSON TAYLOR

My Mind Will Not Entertain **Impure** **Thoughts**

The Truth according to God's Word

"You have heard that it was said, 'You shall not commit adultery.' But I tell you that anyone who looks at a woman lustfully has already committed adultery with her in his heart." (Matt. 5:27 – 28)

Clothe yourselves with the Lord Jesus Christ, and do not think about how to gratify the desires of the flesh. (Rom. 13:14)

We take captive every thought to make it obedient to Christ. (2 Cor. 10:5)

Take up the shield of faith, with which you can extinguish all the flaming arrows of the evil one. (Eph. 6:16)

Whatever is true, whatever is noble, whatever is right, whatever is pure, whatever is lovely, whatever is admirable—if anything is excellent or praiseworthy—think about such things. (Phil. 4:8)

For the grace of God has appeared that offers salvation to all people. It teaches us to say "No" to ungodliness and worldly passions, and to live self-controlled, upright and godly lives in this present age. (Titus 2:11–12)

The Truth

If we're not careful, our minds can attract impure mental images the way a magnet attracts metal. And impure thoughts, lingered on, can lead to impure (and highly regretted) actions. But there's a solution to the problem of impure thoughts: we must actively guard our minds. When a magnet is turned around so the poles are opposite, the magnet actually repels metal. That's what happens when we put a "guard" around our minds. That guard repels impurity and turns the mind to healthier thoughts.

Tell Yourself the Truth

"My mind *does* attract impure thoughts. Therefore I actively guard my mind by not feeding those images from outside sources of impurity (such as pornography or TV shows and movies with sexual innuendo or sexual immorality acted out). When an impure thought comes my way, I repel the idea with the shield of faith—the guardian of my mind. I plant seeds of good thoughts in my mind through reading God's Word and meditating on him and his goodness. When I think of those things, impure thoughts are demagnitized."

Pray the Promise

Lord, so many of my wrong actions—my sins—started with wrong thoughts. I have repented of that and will establish a guard over my thoughts to keep my mind from wandering where it shouldn't go.

Remind me, Lord, when I'm putting myself in a position that might attract impure thoughts.

᭡

"Imagination is the hotbed where this sin is too often hatched. Guard your thoughts, and there will be little fear about your actions."

—J. C. RYLE

My **Inheritance** as a Child of God Can Never Spoil, Perish, or Fade

The Truth according to God's Word

The boundary lines have fallen for me in pleasant places;
surely I have a delightful inheritance. (Ps. 16:6)

"What no eye has seen,
what no ear has heard,
and what no human mind has conceived" —
the things God has prepared for those who love him —
these are the things God has revealed to us by his Spirit.
(1 Cor. 2:9–10)

[Give] joyful thanks to the Father, who has qualified you to share in the inheritance of his holy people in the kingdom of light. (Col. 1:12)

Whatever you do, work at it with all your heart, as working for the Lord, not for human masters, since you know that you will receive an inheritance from the Lord as a reward. (Col. 3:23–24)

Praise be to the God and Father of our Lord Jesus Christ! In his great mercy he has given us new birth into a living hope through the resurrection of Jesus Christ from the dead, and into an inheritance that can never perish, spoil or fade. This inheritance is kept in heaven for you, who through faith are shielded by God's power until the coming of the salvation that is ready to be revealed in the last time. (1 Peter 1:3–5)

The Truth

We Christians are the richest people on earth by virtue of our inheritance as the children of God. It's just that some of our most precious riches are not visible to this world, in fact, they're inconceivable to the human mind. They are, nonetheless, very real—and waiting for us.

Tell Yourself the Truth

"I am the richest person I know. Seriously, I have an inheritance that would put the heirs of Bill Gates or Donald Trump to shame. Although I enjoy part of my inheritance now, the bulk of the estate will be mine in heaven. For now, it is enough to know how very rich I am. It sets me free from envying those who have more of this world's goods."

Pray the Promise

Dear Father in heaven, I revel in my inheritance. Thank you for loving me, for providing for me in this life and the next. Thank you for all the promises included in my inheritance.

⌒

"He that overcometh shall inherit all things. God has no poor children."

— D. L. MOODY

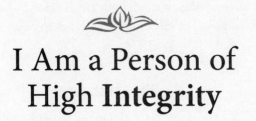

I Am a Person of High Integrity

The Truth according to God's Word

I know, my God, that you test the heart and are pleased with integrity. (1 Chron. 29:17)

May integrity and uprightness protect me, because my hope, LORD, is in you. (Ps. 25:21)

Whoever walks in integrity walks securely, but whoever takes crooked paths will be found out. (Prov. 10:9)

Righteousness guards the person of integrity, but wickedness overthrows the sinner. (Prov. 13:6)

The Truth

God is pleased with integrity. So are other people who see that we are honorable and trustworthy men and women. When we walk in integrity, we honor God—and along the way discover that integrity is its own reward.

Tell Yourself the Truth

"I am a person of strong integrity. I know right from wrong, and I do what's right. Even when others will never see the results—I know God sees. My integrity keeps me secure. I am rewarded in this life and the next for my integrity. I will not allow a stain on my reputation. Such a stain would surely reflect on the Lord too. My good reputation, however, also reflects on the Lord. It gives him the praise he deserves."

Pray the Promise

Thank you, Father, that my integrity speaks volumes to others about the God I serve. May you be honored as I act honorably before others. May you always help me make good decisions and walk in the ways of honesty and righteousness.

❧

"We must be the same person in private and in public. Only the Christian worldview gives us the basis for this kind of integrity."

— CHARLES COLSON

I Exalt the Lord Jesus Christ in My Life

The Truth according to God's Word

Therefore God exalted him to the highest place and gave him the name that is above every name that at the name of Jesus every knee should bow, in heaven and on earth and under the earth, and every tongue acknowledge that Jesus Christ is Lord, to the glory of God the Father. (Phil. 2:9–11)

We pray this so that the name of our Lord Jesus may be glorified in you, and you in him, according to the grace of our God and the Lord Jesus Christ. (2 Thess. 1:12)

Then I looked and heard the voice of many angels, numbering thousands upon thousands, and ten thousand times ten thousand. They encircled the throne and the living creatures and the elders. In a loud voice they were saying:

"Worthy is the Lamb, who was slain,
    to receive power and wealth and wisdom and strength
    and honor and glory and praise!"
Then I heard every creature in heaven and on earth and under
    the earth and on the sea, and all that is in them, saying:
    "To him who sits on the throne and to the Lamb
    be praise and honor and glory and power,
    for ever and ever!" (Rev. 5:11–13)

The Truth

At the very center of God's plan is his love for his Son. It's really all about Jesus. There's only one name at which every knee will eventually bow. But we need not wait until that day to bow in submission and exalt the Lord Jesus Christ. We can do that now. We can "glory" in him today.

Tell Yourself the Truth

"In my imagination, I see ten thousand times ten thousand angels circling the throne of God, praising him by loudly proclaiming, 'Worthy is the Lamb! To him be praise and honor and glory and power, forever and ever!' Then I imagine joining Christians past and present to exalt the Lord Jesus Christ with my mouth and with my service to him. To him be all praise and honor and glory and power forever and ever! May he be glorified in *me*. Praise him!"

Pray the Promise

Lord, when all is said and done, it's all about Jesus, isn't it? He's the only one worthy to receive the praise of creation. And so, Lord, now and forever, I offer up praises to the King of Kings and Lord of Lords; my Redeemer, true Friend, and Master of my life.

⌒

"What think we of Christ? Is he altogether glorious in our eyes, and precious to our hearts? May Christ be our joy, our confidence, our all. May we daily be made more like him, and more devoted to his service."

— MATTHEW HENRY

My Life Is Marked by **Joy**. I Rejoice Always

The Truth according to God's Word

"Do not grieve, for the joy of the LORD is your strength." (Neh. 8:10)

You make known to me the path of life;
    you will fill me with joy in your presence. (Ps. 16:11)

My heart leaps for joy,
    and with my song I praise him. (Ps. 28:7)

"Those the LORD has rescued will return.
    They will enter Zion with singing;
    everlasting joy will crown their heads.
    Gladness and joy will overtake them,
    and sorrow and sighing will flee away." (Isa. 51:11)

Rejoice in the Lord always. I will say it again: Rejoice! (Phil. 4:4)

Though you have not seen him, you love him; and even though you do not see him now, you believe in him and are filled with an inexpressible and glorious joy, for you are receiving the end result of your faith, the salvation of your souls. (1 Peter 1:8–9)

The Truth

Joy is one of the hallmarks of a mature Christian because as believers, we live in God's presence where there is *always, always, always* an abundance of joy. The joy of the Lord is our strength. No joy, no strength. Be joyful and be strong.

Tell Yourself the Truth

"Jesus promised that my joy would be complete, not partial. I find my joy made complete in his presence. It isn't possible to contemplate Christ and my salvation without responding in joy. Joy, too, is a fruit of the Holy Spirit. I have the Holy Spirit, thus I have the Spirit's joy. When I feel weak, I remember that the joy of the Lord is my strength, and I make a decision to be joyful and strengthened."

Pray the Promise

Increase my joy, Lord! May people see me and wonder at the deep-seated joy I have. May my heart sing with your joyful praises even during the "down" times in my life. Thank you, Lord, for giving me your joy! Thank you for joyful strength.

⌇

"Begin to rejoice in the Lord, and your bones will flourish like an herb, and your cheeks will glow with the bloom of health and freshness. Worry, fear, distrust, care — all are poisonous! Joy is balm and healing, and if you will but rejoice, God will give power."

— A. B. SIMPSON

In Christ I Am Free from Religious **Legalism**

The Truth according to God's Word

He has made us competent as ministers of a new covenant — not of the letter but of the Spirit; for the letter kills, but the Spirit gives life. (2 Cor. 3:6)

You, my brothers and sisters, were called to be free. But do not use your freedom to indulge the flesh; rather, serve one another humbly in love. For the entire law is fulfilled in keeping this one command: "Love your neighbor as yourself." (Gal. 5:13 – 14)

The Truth

The fruit of a life rooted in God is doing good. But if we're trying to please God by doing good works without fully trusting in the finished work of Christ, our good deeds are for nothing. And if we think we please God by obeying a list of dos and don'ts, we're caught up in a form of legalism that kills. Let's stop trusting in our good deeds and trust only in Christ. Then we can see what real fruit looks like.

Tell Yourself the Truth

"Sometimes I feel like I should try to please God by reading my Bible more or praying harder. If I miss church, I feel like God is disappointed in me. But I know that it is only by God's grace that I'm saved and only by that same grace that I am approved of by God. I will not allow legalism to smother my life in Christ. Rather, by letting Christ live through me, I will enjoy the abundant Spirit-filled life."

Pray the Promise

Oh Lord! Thank you for freedom in Christ! What a terrible bondage is religious legalism by which I can never please you. I pray that I grow in grace and walk more abundantly in your Spirit — your life-giving Spirit. What joy you give me as the shackles of legalism fall from me and I delight in you and what you've done, not what I can do.

Praise you, Father!

❧

"Trying to work for God without worshiping God results in joyless legalism. Work minus worship magnifies your will power not God's worth. If you try to do things for God without delighting in God, you bring dishonor upon God. Serving God without savoring God is lifeless and unreal."

— JOHN PIPER

Loneliness Holds Value. God Is My Companion

The Truth according to God's Word

Turn to me and be gracious to me,
for I am lonely and afflicted. (Ps. 25:16)

But Jesus often withdrew to lonely places and prayed. (Luke 5:16)

"A time is coming and in fact has come when you will be scattered, each to your own home. You will leave me all alone. Yet I am not alone, for my Father is with me." (John 16:32)

"Never will I leave you;
never will I forsake you." (Heb. 13:5)

The Truth

Early in the Bible we read that it is not good for man to be alone. For that reason, marriage was given. But not all are married. Many live by themselves and are lonely for companionship. Even many who are married are lonely. To the lonely, God would say to draw close to him and he will be your companion, and by virtue of drawing close to him, you will soon find yourself drawing closer to others who have put him first. Consider, too, that Jesus went to lonely places in order to pray. If God has set you in a lonely place, perhaps that's your call to follow Jesus' example and be one who excels in prayer.

To those who know someone who is lonely, God would say, "In befriending the lonely, you befriend me."

Tell Yourself the Truth

"I can never be truly lonely; God is always with me. He is always my companion and always loves me. He will never leave me nor forsake me. I will take note of those around me who may be lonely and will reach out to them. In so doing, I reach out to Jesus. And if it is God's will to keep me for himself in this life, it will be a call to pray and befriend others who may also feel lonely."

Pray the Promise

Lord, you know I'm so tired of being lonely. I do love you, but I'd love some other person in my life to share good times and conversation with. You know that need, just as you know all my needs. I trust you to fill that need by sending me friends or to so fill me with your companionship that I will no longer realize I'm lonely. Thank you, Father, for friends. Thank you for your Holy Spirit living within me.

∽

"Loneliness comes over us sometimes as a sudden tide. It is one of the terms of our humanness, and, in a sense, therefore, incurable. Yet I have found peace in my loneliest times not only through acceptance of the situation, but through making it an offering to God, who can transfigure it into something for the good of others."

— ELISABETH ELLIOT

Love One Another

The Truth according to God's Word

"A new command I give you: Love one another. As I have loved you, so you must love one another. By this everyone will know that you are my disciples, if you love one another." (John 13:34–35)

"This is my command: Love each other." (John 15:17)

Be devoted to one another in love. Honor one another above yourselves. (Rom. 12:10)

Do everything in love. (1 Cor. 16:14)

Now about your love for one another we do not need to write to you, for you yourselves have been taught by God to love each other. (1 Thess. 4:9)

The Truth

Loving others, says Jesus, is the second commandment only to loving God with all our heart, soul, mind, and strength. Paul says we are taught by God to love one another, and he urges us to "do everything in love." Our love for each other is the sign that we really do know God. But for it to function as a sign, it must be seen by those watching us.

Tell Yourself the Truth

"Loving others is the God-designed outlet for loving God. When I love someone I can see, it proves I love the one I cannot see. I am compelled by God's love to be a lover of all the people I meet—even when loving others may hurt me or cost me something I hold dear. My love for others compels me to reach out to them, even sacrificially, as Christ did."

Pray the Promise

Lord, teach me to love others more deeply. Not just in word, but in action too. Let my love be a sign to others that I belong to you. Let there be no mistake that the gift of love is functioning in me.

⌒

"Our love to God is measured by our everyday fellowship with others and the love it displays."

— ANDREW MURRAY

God Has Never Ceased Doing **Miracles**. He is the Same Yesterday, Today, and Forever

The Truth according to God's Word

You are the God who performs miracles;
  you display your power among the peoples. (Ps. 77:14)

And he did not do many miracles there because of their lack of faith. (Matt. 13:58)

So again I ask, does God give you his Spirit and work miracles among you by the works of the law, or by your believing what you heard? (Gal. 3:5)

The Truth

God *never* changes. He is the same yesterday, today, and forever. His power and might are just as potent today as they were when Jesus walked the earth. Miracles do happen. And we must, must, must continually believe God for miracles. Let it never be said of us, "He did not do many miracles there because of their lack of faith."

Tell Yourself the Truth

"My God is a miraculous God. Even this very life of mine is a miracle. God can do anything—naturally or supernaturally. Nothing is beyond him. His miracle power is active in my life and in my circumstances. Let the skeptics debate all they want. But when nothing but a miracle will do, I trust God to provide one."

Pray the Promise

God, the notion that you can't or won't move in miraculous ways today can be translated into "he did not do many miracles there because of their lack of faith." Lord, give me faith to see miracles when only a miracle will do.

∽

"How quickly we forget God's great deliverances in our lives. How easily we take for granted the miracles he performed in our past."

— DAVID WILKERSON

God Is Lord of My **Money** Too

The Truth according to God's Word

Whoever loves money never has enough;
   whoever loves wealth is never satisfied with their income. (Eccl. 5:10)

"No one can serve two masters. Either you will hate the one and love the other, or you will be devoted to the one and despise the other. You cannot serve both God and money." (Luke 16:13)

Give to everyone what you owe them: If you owe taxes, pay taxes; if revenue, then revenue; if respect, then respect; if honor, then honor. Let no debt remain outstanding, except the continuing debt to love one another, for whoever loves others has fulfilled the law. (Rom. 13:7–8)

The love of money is a root of all kinds of evil. Some people, eager for money, have wandered from the faith and pierced themselves with many griefs. (1 Tim. 6:10)

Keep your lives free from the love of money and be content with what you have, because God has said, "Never will I leave you; never will I forsake you." (Heb. 13:5)

The Truth

Money, properly used, is a tool. Improperly used, it is an idol. Those who make the accumulation of money their goal are headed in the wrong direction. Money, like our very lives, is to be invested in God's kingdom, not wasted or spent foolishly. Nor should we go into debt. We are to owe no debt except to love another. Money is a trust from God. Use it wisely.

Tell Yourself the Truth

"I am responsible with money. Money is not my goal and not my god. My Lord supplies my needs and many of my wants too. I seek first his kingdom, and all the other things in life are added to me. I count my spiritual assets as more important than my material goods. And when I think of investing, I think of it in terms of how my life might be better invested in God's kingdom. Money comes and money goes, but the investments I make in God's kingdom are eternal. I take my financial advice from the Bible and avoid debt whenever possible. I will work to extricate myself from my present debts and unwise investments. I will live by Christian financial principles — being a giver, not a taker, owing only the debt of love to others."

Pray the Promise

God of my life, I trust you with my finances. You are the source of my income and always will be. Help me see my money first in the way it can be used for your kingdom. As I prove faithful in money matters, I vow to continue being a channel for money to flow to the places it needs to be. Thank you for using me as a way to bless others who have less than I do.

Lord, guide me in making the decisions that will bring me out of debt quickly. Put my finances on an even keel so I'm not tempted to borrow to pay for things I don't even really need. Help me to seek your prosperity, Lord, and not that of this world.

⌇

"Water is useful to the ship and helps it to sail better to the haven, but let the water get into the ship, if it is not pumped out, it drowns the ship. So riches are useful and convenient for our passage. We sail more comfortably with them through the troubles of this world; but if the water gets into the ship, if love of riches gets into the heart, then we are drowned by them."

— THOMAS WATSON

I Am a **New Creation** in Christ

The Truth according to God's Word

Jesus replied, "Very truly I tell you, no one can see the kingdom of God unless they are born again." (John 3:3)

Therefore, if anyone is in Christ, the new creation has come: The old has gone, the new is here! (2 Cor. 5:17)

Neither circumcision nor uncircumcision means anything; what counts is the new creation. (Gal. 6:15)

Do not lie to each other, since you have taken off your old self with its practices and have put on the new self, which is being renewed in knowledge in the image of its Creator. (Col. 3:9 – 10)

The Truth

At the moment of salvation — of being born again — we're given a new nature. Paul referred to it as becoming a "new creation." As we live in the power of this new nature, we grow in the Christian life. The new creation keeps us from sin and anxiety, and it gives us boldness and courage. We are enabled to be all we're meant to be because of the power of our new nature.

Tell Yourself the Truth

"Old things in my life have passed away. All things have become new. I now live by the new nature I was given at my new birth. In my new nature, I find every resource I need for every life situation. I overcome all obstacles by declaring my old nature dead and relying on my new heavenly nature. Through this nature God has given me, I walk confidently in the Spirit, I avoid sin, I live in unity with other believers, and I live loving and serving God. My life now is one of constantly discovering more and more about the power of this new nature."

Pray the Promise

Thank you, Father, that when I came to faith in you, I was made into a new creation. Truly the old has passed away, and I now live moment by moment as a totally new "born-again" person. With that new creation came the power to live a full productive life, pleasing to you. Thank you for watching over me, Lord, as I daily walk out that divine life that's mine. Praise you, Lord!

~

"To be born again is, as it were, to enter upon a new existence, to have a new mind, a new heart, new views, new principles, new tastes, new affections, new likings, new dislikings, new fears, new joys, new sorrows, new love to things once hated, new hatred to things once loved, new thoughts of God, and ourselves, and the world, and the life to come, and salvation."

—J. C. RYLE

I Stand against the Power of the **Occult** in My Life

The Truth according to God's Word

"'Do not turn to mediums or seek out spiritists, for you will be defiled by them. I am the LORD your God.'" (Lev. 19:31)

When someone tells you to consult mediums and spiritists, who whisper and mutter, should not a people inquire of their God? Why consult the dead on behalf of the living? (Isa. 8:19)

Once when we were going to the place of prayer, we were met by a female slave who had a spirit by which she predicted the future. She earned a great deal of money for her owners by fortune-telling. She followed Paul and the rest of us, shouting, "These men are servants of the Most High God, who are telling you the way to be saved." She kept this up for many days. Finally Paul became so annoyed that he turned around and said to the spirit, "In the name of Jesus Christ I command you to come out of her!" At that moment the spirit left her. (Acts 16:16–18)

The Truth

One of Satan's more overt attempts to capture the hearts and minds of people is through occult activity. Examples include astrology, consultations with mediums, witchcraft, Ouija boards, and the many deceptive spiritual enticements available today. One "innocent" occult activity usually leads to deeper darkness. We can't be ignorant of Satan's devices. We're children of light, and we need to stay away from all forms of spiritual darkness, rejecting them soundly. They must have no part in our lives.

Tell Yourself the Truth

"I am not ignorant of Satan's strategies to pull me away from Christ. They will not succeed. I renounce every occult practice in my past and rebuke satanic forces that entice me into darkness. *They cannot have me.* I firmly and fully belong to Christ; Satan has no further claim on this child of God. As forcefully as I reject all occult activity and temptations, I also forcefully rely on the power of God to overcome these powers of darkness that want me. I reject any spiritual influences that would tell me lies about who I am or whom I belong to. I reject the devil, and he must flee. I do not fear Satan; rather, he must now fear me. I stand firmly with the Lord against all the bondages of my past. His blood covers me, and Satan dare not go there—indeed he cannot. There is no room in my life or my home for evil practices. I am fully a child of the light, not of the darkness."

Pray the Promise

Lord, I repent of the past occult practices in my life. I renounce them all and rebuke the darkness that has accompanied them. God, you must be my fortress against all of Satan's occult schemes to tempt me. Thank you for your powerful deliverance.

∽

"There is no neutral ground in the universe; every square inch, every split second, is claimed by God and counter-claimed by Satan."

— C. S. LEWIS

God Gives Me Opportunities I Never Expected

The Truth according to God's Word

Therefore, as we have opportunity, let us do good to all people, especially to those who belong to the family of believers. (Gal. 6:10)

Be very careful, then, how you live—not as unwise but as wise, making the most of every opportunity, because the days are evil. Therefore do not be foolish, but understand what the Lord's will is. (Eph. 5:15–17)

Be wise in the way you act toward outsiders; make the most of every opportunity. (Col. 4:5)

The Truth

Opportunity is God's open door. Don't just stand at the threshold; walk in and seize that which God is offering.

Tell Yourself the Truth

"I move ahead with God. I watch for his open doors—his opportunities—to take the next step in my destiny. God will make every opportunity so clear that I won't miss it. And when he does, I will summon the courage and walk through that open door boldly, eager to see what is waiting for me on the other side."

Pray the Promise

Father God, I thank you for being the God of new opportunities. Whether they're in my workplace, my church, my family, or somewhere else, I welcome them. I pray over each one to make sure it's from you, and then I step forward with confidence. Lord, I pray you'll keep opening more doors for me and granting me both the wisdom to recognize your opportunities and the ability to make the most of them.

⁓

"God is preparing his heroes. And when the opportunity comes, he can fit them into their places in a moment. And the world will wonder where they came from."

— A. B. SIMPSON

My **Past** Is *Past*

The Truth according to God's Word

"Forget the former things;
    do not dwell on the past.
    See, I am doing a new thing!
    Now it springs up; do you not perceive it?
    I am making a way in the wilderness
    and streams in the wasteland." (Isa. 43:18–19)

And we know that in all things God works for the good of those who love him, who have been called according to his purpose. (Rom. 8:28)

Brothers and sisters, I do not consider myself yet to have taken hold of it. But one thing I do: Forgetting what is behind and straining toward what is ahead, I press on toward the goal to win the prize for which God has called me heavenward in Christ Jesus. (Phil. 3:13–14)

The Truth

Success in life is learning never to be afraid of the past — or the future. The past is dead. There is no life there. How then can we allow something long dead to rule our lives today? We must stop carrying around the dead weight of a past that no longer exists. God has moved on with us from our past. Shouldn't we also?

There is one comfort we can take from our past, however. We can know that among the hidden ways God works is his ability to take our past—no matter how sad or sordid—and turn it into good. What once were stumbling blocks, God turns into stepping-stones. If you have doubts, ask some of the great failures of the Bible: Abraham, Rahab, David, Moses, Jonah, and Peter. Their dubious pasts gave way to God's plan for redeemed futures.

It's time to stop replaying the tape of our past mistakes and reliving the feelings that bring despair and hopelessness. It's time to look up and move on, entrusting God with that which lies behind.

Tell Yourself the Truth

"My past is gone. The sins from years ago and from yesterday have been forgiven and forgotten by God. I live in the present, looking expectantly to the future. I don't allow my past to influence the joy and success God means for me to have now. What I count as a bad memory, God can use for my good. I will not relive or resent my past. It now belongs to God."

Pray the Promise

Lord, sometimes my past sins come back to bite me. Either I remember them with pain or the enemy uses them to accuse me and assure me that my future is rooted in my past. But, Lord, my true future is rooted not in my past, but in you. Thank you for taking all the pain of my irreparable past and putting it behind us both. Now I will be free from that pain—even the worst of it (and you know what that is, Lord), and I can have a happy, irresistible future rooted firmly in you.

~

"Let the past sleep, but let it sleep on the bosom of Christ. Leave the Irreparable Past in his hands, and step out into the Irresistible Future with him."

— OSWALD CHAMBERS

God Brings the Best to Those Who Are **Patient**. I Will Wait on the Lord

The Truth according to God's Word

Be still before the LORD
and wait patiently for him. (Ps. 37:7)

Whoever is patient has great understanding,
but one who is quick-tempered displays folly. (Prov. 14:29)

Be joyful in hope, patient in affliction, faithful in prayer. (Rom. 12:12)

The Truth

God is patient with us. We must also be patient as he works out the details of our lives. He sees the entire canvas; we see only the brushstrokes of today. Wait and behold the full picture—in due time. There is power in patience.

Tell Yourself the Truth

"I can say I trust God all day long, but the proof is in my ability to wait patiently for his will to unfold in *his* time, not mine. I give

God room enough and time enough to create the masterpiece that is my life. I know there is no good thing meant for me that will not come to me if I but pray, give thanks, and wait for the right time — God's time. It is far better to let God take his time to make me into a strong redwood tree than to allow me to shoot up like bamboo, only to disappear after a short season."

Pray the Promise

Lord, you have something in mind for me that requires patience on my part. Therefore I will pray, rejoice, and give thanks while I wait patiently. Good things will come to me from your hand. Take your time, Lord. I'll wait.

～

"There is nothing which so certifies the genuineness of a man's faith as his patience and his patient endurance, his keeping on steadily in spite of everything."

MARTYN LLOYD-JONES

Great **Peace** Have Those Who Belong to the Lord

The Truth according to God's Word

The Lord blesses his people with peace. (Ps. 29:11)

Great peace have those who love your law,
    and nothing can make them stumble. (Ps. 119:165)

You will keep in perfect peace
    those whose minds are steadfast,
    because they trust in you. (Isa. 26:3)

"Peace I leave with you; my peace I give you. I do not give to you as the world gives. Do not let your hearts be troubled and do not be afraid." (John 14:27)

Let the peace of Christ rule in your hearts, since as members of one body you were called to peace. (Col. 3:15)

The Truth

Peace isn't the absence of tension. It's the presence of God in the midst of tension.

Tell Yourself the Truth

"Jesus has left me with his peace—a peace that can't be found in the world—therefore I'm not troubled by the stress in my life. God works on my behalf, and so I have peace today and in every situation. Peace is my daily companion. Peace remains with me despite the noise around me. Jesus' peace is my peace. Nothing can stress me or make me anxious."

Pray the Promise

Father, your Word promises great peace to those who love your law. You say nothing can make them stumble. Natural-born stumbler that I am, I look to Jesus as the one who fulfilled the law for me and is thus the bringer of my peace.

Father, you also say you will give great peace to those who keep their minds stayed on you. That, then, is my way to a peaceful mind. Lord, I do stay my mind on you in all circumstances.

∽

"A great many people are trying to make peace, but that has already been done. God has not left it for us to do; all we have to do is to enter into it."

—D. L. Moody

I Accept as a Blessing **Persecution** for Living a Godly Life

The Truth according to God's Word

"Blessed are those who are persecuted because of righteousness, for theirs is the kingdom of heaven.

"Blessed are you when people insult you, persecute you and falsely say all kinds of evil against you because of me." (Matt. 5:10 – 11)

"But I tell you, love your enemies and pray for those who persecute you." (Matt. 5:44)

"Remember what I told you: 'A servant is not greater than his master.' If they persecuted me, they will persecute you also." (John 15:20)

Everyone who wants to live a godly life in Christ Jesus will be persecuted. (2 Tim. 3:12)

The Truth

John Foxe, author of the classic *Foxe's Book of Martyrs*, reports that the persecution of Christians began with Nero in AD 67. Since then, Christians somewhere have always been maligned for their faith, often by those who formerly were their friends and often even by close relatives. Persecution is something every Christian should expect to encounter at some time in life. Of course, in many countries around the world, Christians are put to death for their faith. Most of us, however, will not likely see that degree of persecution. But no matter the level of persecution, our reaction should be rejoicing. For when we are persecuted for our faith, Jesus says we are being blessed. Persecution refines and tests our faith.

Tell Yourself the Truth

"My firm faith in Christ will inevitably lead to persecution on some level, from my family or friends, at school or on the job. I am ready for that. I will count it all joy when I'm ridiculed or belittled for my faith. The apostle Paul was a great persecutor of the faith before he came to know Christ. I pray that some of those who reject me and make fun of me for my faith will yet come to Christ. Until then, no amount of persecution can separate me from the one who was persecuted and put to death for my sins. It's an honor to endure what small persecutions come my way, just for the joy of following in the footsteps of those persecuted before me — and to be in the company of my Teacher, Friend, and Savior. I accept rejection and persecution as part of my inheritance as a Christian, and I make it a practice to pray for the persecuted church in other parts of the world. May God give them more grace."

Pray the Promise

God, my prayer is for all Christians worldwide who face persecution. Keep them strong in their faith. Encourage them by your Spirit. Give them release from oppression. Save them from torture. Be with them in death. May their crown be waiting when they cross into heaven. As for me, may my reactions to personal persecution be godly reactions, not malicious or angry—or worst of all, compromise and backing down from what I believe.

⚬

"To be right with God has often meant to be in trouble with men."

— A. W. TOZER

I Am Committed to Helping the **Poor**. In So Doing, I Am Lending to the Lord

The Truth according to God's Word

Whoever oppresses the poor shows contempt for their Maker,
   but whoever is kind to the needy honors God. (Prov. 14:31)

Whoever is kind to the poor lends to the LORD,
   and he will reward them for what they have done. (Prov. 19:17)

Whoever shuts their ears to the cry of the poor
   will also cry out and not be answered. (Prov. 21:13)

In Joppa there was a disciple named Tabitha ... she was always doing good and helping the poor. (Acts 9:36)

If anyone has material possessions and sees a brother or sister in need but has no pity on them, how can the love of God be in that person? Dear children, let us not love with words or speech but with actions and in truth. (1 John 3:17 – 18)

The Truth

Jesus walks this earth today. He's disguised as the poor, broken, and lonely. When we minister to these, we touch Jesus. Scripture goes so far as to say that when we give to the poor, we're lending to God. Contrarily, no matter how long we've been a Christian, the moment we have forgotten the poor, we have become spiritually impoverished ourselves.

Tell Yourself the Truth

"The poor are always on God's heart, therefore I make sure they're on my heart. I prayerfully follow God's leading in reaching the poor. I give, I pray, I offer up my hands and my feet to the poor. In so doing, I offer these to Jesus. I never judge the poor or assign blame to them for their condition. My only concern is the Lord's concern: that they be remembered and fed."

Pray the Promise

God, give me new eyes to see the poor around me. They are my responsibility. When I see the poor, may I also see you standing in their shoes.

~

"What does love look like? It has the hands to help others. It has the feet to hasten to the poor and needy. It has eyes to see misery and want. It has the ears to hear the sighs and sorrows of men. That is what love looks like."

— AUGUSTINE

The **Praise** of God Is Always on My Lips

The Truth according to God's Word

I will proclaim the name of the LORD.
   Oh, praise the greatness of our God! (Deut. 32:3)

"The LORD lives! Praise be to my Rock!
   Exalted be my God, the Rock, my Savior!" (2 Sam. 22:47)

Early in the morning they left for the Desert of Tekoa. As they set out, Jehoshaphat stood and said, "Listen to me, Judah and people of Jerusalem! Have faith in the LORD your God and you will be upheld; have faith in his prophets and you will be successful." After consulting the people, Jehoshaphat appointed men to sing to the LORD and to praise him for the splendor of his holiness as they went out at the head of the army, saying:

   "Give thanks to the LORD,
      for his love endures forever."

As they began to sing and praise, the LORD set ambushes against the men of Ammon and Moab and Mount Seir who were invading Judah, and they were defeated. (2 Chron. 20:20–22)

Praise the LORD.
Praise God in his sanctuary;
    praise him in his mighty heavens.
Praise him for his acts of power;
    praise him for his surpassing greatness.
Praise him with the sounding of the trumpet,
    praise him with the harp and lyre,
praise him with timbrel and dancing,
    praise him with the strings and pipe,
praise him with the clash of cymbals,
    praise him with resounding cymbals.
Let everything that has breath praise the LORD.
Praise the LORD. (Ps. 150)

Through Jesus, therefore, let us continually offer to God a sacrifice of praise—the fruit of lips that openly profess his name. (Heb. 13:15)

But you are a chosen people, a royal priesthood, a holy nation, God's special possession, that you may declare the praises of him who called you out of darkness into his wonderful light. (1 Peter 2:9)

The Truth

Jehoshaphat knew the secret to victory. He sent the praisers out ahead of the army. As they worshiped the Lord with their lips, their victory over the invaders was swift and complete. When we have invaders in our lives, sending out praise ahead will win the day. In every situation, our lips should show forth God's praise. We have much to praise God about. *Much.*

Tell Yourself the Truth

"I am a praiser! I delight to worship my God in words and song. Each day his goodness to me causes me to rise up and give him the praise and glory he deserves. He is my Rock, my high tower, my fortress. My praises give wings to the burdens in my life. Forever I will be praising my God!"

Pray the Promise

Lord, help me to remember to keep praise for you always on my lips— no words of wanting this or that or complaining about my lot. It's just good to sit before you and praise you, not asking for anything. For at such times, I truly need nothing more.

⸜

"If you had a thousand crowns you should put them all on the head of Christ! And if you had a thousand tongues they should all sing his praise, for he is worthy!"

— WILLIAM TIPTAFT

There Is No Power on Earth Greater Than My **Prayers**

The Truth according to God's Word

Evening and morning and at noon
    I will pray, and cry aloud,
    And He shall hear my voice. (Ps. 55:17 NKJV)

"I will do whatever you ask in my name, so that the Father may be glorified in the Son. You may ask me for anything in my name, and I will do it." (John 14:13 – 14)

In the same way, the Spirit helps us in our weakness. We do not know what we ought to pray for, but the Spirit himself intercedes for us through wordless groans. (Rom. 8:26)

Devote yourselves to prayer, being watchful and thankful. (Col. 4:2)

This is the confidence we have in approaching God: that if we ask anything according to his will, he hears us. And if we know that he hears us — whatever we ask — we know that we have what we asked of him. (1 John 5:14 – 15)

And when he had taken it, the four living creatures and the twenty-four elders fell down before the Lamb. Each one had a harp and they were holding golden bowls full of incense, which are the prayers of God's people. (Rev. 5:8)

The Truth

The Bible is chock-full of admonitions and encouragements to pray. We're told to pray without ceasing, to pray with persistence, to pray in faith, to pray with the right motives, to pray in confidence, to pray in Jesus' name, and so on.

It's no surprise that much is made of prayer in the Bible. Prayer is our lifeline to God. It's our heavenly Father's gift to us, our means of communicating with him. Prayer is right smack dab at the center of the Christian life. How much more then should we be on our knees, even on our faces, before our great God?

Prayer is no ritual; it's a loving exchange between Father and child. Why then would we *not* pray? Especially when we realize the vast power our prayers have on circumstances and on our very lives. If our lives are powerless, we must also ask ourselves, are they also prayerless?

Tell Yourself the Truth

"My prayers have power because the God of the universes hears and answers my every plea. Daily I raise my voice in prayers of thanksgiving, praise, adoration, petition, and intercession. My prayers are a joy to God. He delights in my prayers and bids me pray often, asking what I will, just as children ask their fathers for what they need and want. Prayer is at the center of my life. I live in the spirit of prayer!"

Pray the Promise

Thank you, Lord, for prayer. I love that I can come to you anytime and anyplace and know that you eagerly (not grudgingly) hear and will answer my prayers. I stake everything in my life on your faithfulness in prayer. May my prayers be a sweet incense to you, O Lord.

᠊᠊᠊ᦧ᠊᠊᠊

"I live in the spirit of prayer. I pray as I walk about, when I lie down and when I rise up. And the answers are always coming. Thousands and tens of thousands of times have my prayers been answered. When once I am persuaded that a thing is right and for the glory of God, I go on praying for it until the answer comes. George Mueller never gives up!"

— GEORGE MUELLER

God's **Promises** Are More Valuable Than Gold, and They Are Mine

The Truth according to God's Word

Not one of all the LORD's good promises to Israel failed; every one was fulfilled. (Josh. 21:45)

Your promises have been thoroughly tested,
    and your servant loves them. (Ps. 119:140)

The LORD is trustworthy in all he promises
    and faithful in all he does. (Ps. 145:13)

Yet [Abraham] did not waver through unbelief regarding the promise of God, but was strengthened in his faith and gave glory to God, being fully persuaded that God had power to do what he had promised. (Rom. 4:20–21)

For no matter how many promises God has made, they are "Yes" in Christ. (2 Cor. 1:20)

His divine power has given us everything we need for a godly life through our knowledge of him who called us by his own glory and goodness. Through these he has given us his very great and precious promises, so that through them you may participate in the divine nature, having escaped the corruption in the world caused by evil desires. (2 Peter 1:3–4)

The Truth

God's promises are bread to us; we live on them. And God is faithful to keep his promises to us. Those who do not believe the promises of God cannot enjoy them. If we're not seeing the promises of God at work in our lives, perhaps we're looking through unbelieving eyes.

Tell Yourself the Truth

"God gives me promises in the Word so that I can grow into a fully mature Christian by being 'a partaker of his divine nature' and thereby escape the 'corruption in the world.' God gives me promises that I can apply to my life as I believe them, say them, pray them, and then live them out. The promises of God shape my being and give me confidence when I face trials. The promises of God are more precious than gold to me. Never yet has a promise of God failed me, nor will it ever. The promises of God are my insurance for this life and the next."

Pray the Promise

Dear Father, thank you for the promises in your Word. Thank you that none can be broken because each is backed up by your character. Never will I take your promises for granted; nor will I ever use them for selfish motives, but always as a way of glorifying you in my life. Show me, Lord, more of the precious promises in your Word, and I will put them to good use.

⌒

"God's promises were never meant to be thrown aside as waste paper. He intended that they should be used. God's gold is not miser's money, but is minted to be traded with. Nothing pleases our Lord better than to see his promises put into circulation. He loves to see his children bring them up to him, and say, 'Lord, do as Thou hast said!' Our heavenly Banker delights to cash his own notes. Never let the promise rust. Draw the sword of promise out of its scabbard and use it with holy violence!"

— CHARLES SPURGEON

God Delights in **Prospering** Me

The Truth according to God's Word

Blessed is the one
   who does not walk in step with the wicked
   or stand in the way that sinners take
   or sit in the company of mockers,
   but whose delight is in the law of the LORD,
   and who meditates on his law day and night.
   That person is like a tree planted by streams of water,
   which yields its fruit in season
   and whose leaf does not wither —
   whatever they do prospers. (Ps. 1:1 – 3)

The LORD will guide you always;
   he will satisfy your needs in a sun-scorched land
   and will strengthen your frame.
   You will be like a well-watered garden,
   like a spring whose waters never fail. (Isa. 58:11)

The Truth

Prosperity for the Christian is not measured by material goods but by how well he or she is living out God's destiny. Is there fruit in the life? The fruit is the measure of God's prosperity.

Tell Yourself the Truth

"God is the source of my prosperity. Because I delight in his law, I'm like a tree planted by streams of water. I yield fruit in due season; my leaf does not wither—and whatever I do prospers."

Pray the Promise

Lord God, on my own, I would fail at all I do. But by relying on your promises, I prosper in all I do. Thank you for where you've planted me—by a stream of living water that nourishes me and brings fruit out of life—abundant fruit at that. Lord, my goal is that my prosperity overflows to others around me.

∽

"When a man becomes a Christian, he becomes industrious, trustworthy, and prosperous."

—JOHN WESLEY

I Am Safe in God's Hands. His Divine **Protection** Is Always with Me

The Truth according to God's Word

The LORD is my rock, my fortress and my deliverer;
    my God is my rock, in whom I take refuge,
    my shield and the horn of my salvation, my stronghold.
    (Ps. 18:2)

You are my hiding place;
    you will protect me from trouble
    and surround me with songs of deliverance. (Ps. 32:7)

Whoever dwells in the shelter of the Most High
    will rest in the shadow of the Almighty.
I will say of the LORD, "He is my refuge and my fortress,
    my God, in whom I trust."
Surely he will save you
    from the fowler's snare
    and from the deadly pestilence.
He will cover you with his feathers,
    and under his wings you will find refuge;
    his faithfulness will be your shield and rampart.

You will not fear the terror of night,
    nor the arrow that flies by day,
nor the pestilence that stalks in the darkness,
    nor the plague that destroys at midday.
A thousand may fall at your side,
    ten thousand at your right hand,
    but it will not come near you.
You will only observe with your eyes
    and see the punishment of the wicked.
If you say, "The LORD is my refuge,"
    and you make the Most High your dwelling,
no harm will overtake you,
    no disaster will come near your tent.
For he will command his angels concerning you
    to guard you in all your ways;
they will lift you up in their hands,
    so that you will not strike your foot against a stone.
You will tread on the lion and the cobra;
    you will trample the great lion and the serpent.
"Because he loves me," says the LORD, "I will rescue him;
    I will protect him, for he acknowledges my name.
He will call on me, and I will answer him;
    I will be with him in trouble,
    I will deliver him and honor him.
With long life I will satisfy him
    and show him my salvation." (Ps. 91)

The LORD will keep you from all harm—
    he will watch over your life. (Ps. 121:7)

"Holy Father, protect them by the power of your name, the name
you gave me, so that they may be one as we are one." (John 17:11)

The Truth

The need to feel protected from danger or the unknown is a natural response. We don't have to learn how to be afraid. But we do have to learn how to be *un*afraid. Faith in his promises is the way God wants us to learn how to rely on his protection. There are many promises of protection in the Bible, but perhaps the gold mine of protection promises is found in Psalm 91. We would each do well to memorize it so that it is on our tongues in times of need. It reminds us that when danger is near, God is nearer yet.

Tell Yourself the Truth

"I will not fear danger. God is always with me, even in the darkest situations. He has a hedge of protection around me that no one — not even Satan — can pierce. God is always on the alert to impending danger and either warns me or protects me in ways I'm unaware of. With God's protection, I'm safe from harm."

Pray the Promise

O God, who will protect me against danger? Only you! You are my shield against all that would harm me. You put a hedge of protection around me, guarding me against the enemy's arrows, shot in the form of dangerous situations. Keep me close, Lord. Closer yet.

PROTECTION

"One day after a long journey, I rested in front of a house. Suddenly a sparrow came towards me, blown helplessly by a strong wind. From another direction, an eagle dived to catch the panicky sparrow. Threatened from different directions, the sparrow flew into my lap. By choice, it would not normally do that. However, the little bird was seeking for a refuge from a great danger. Likewise, the violent winds of suffering and trouble blow us into the Lord's protective hands."

— SADHU SUNDAR SINGH

I May Experience **Rejection** on Earth, but There Is Only Acceptance for Those Who Are in Christ

The Truth according to God's Word

"The LORD himself goes before you and will be with you; he will never leave you nor forsake you. Do not be afraid; do not be discouraged." (Deut. 31:8)

"For the sake of his great name the LORD will not reject his people, because the LORD was pleased to make you his own." (1 Sam. 12:22)

Though my father and mother forsake me,
    the LORD will receive me. (Ps. 27:10)

For the LORD loves the just
    and will not forsake his faithful ones. (Ps. 37:28)

"Can a mother forget the baby at her breast
    and have no compassion on the child she has borne?
    Though she may forget,

I will not forget you!
See, I have engraved you on the palms of my hands;
your walls are ever before me." (Isa. 49:15 – 16)

The Truth

Rejection hurts in the extreme. Some people never fully recover from being rejected. I suppose at one time or another almost everyone faces rejection from someone. It's how we respond that determines what we're made of. Do we keep that rejection alive and festering, giving it power over us, or do we reject rejection?

Sometimes our experiences of rejection go back many years, perhaps even to our childhood, resulting in scars that carry into adulthood. Sometimes we're rejected as adults by a spouse or friend we trusted. We may even be rejected by fellow Christians we've known and trusted for years. Here on earth, rejection can happen anywhere. But among God's people, there should be no fear of rejection when we realize that he will never leave us nor forsake us. Our love and acceptance by God should (and will) heal any earthly rejection we suffer. After all, we follow the Man who has known the severest rejection of all.

Tell Yourself the Truth

"Rejection hurts. I know that pain from experience. But in Christ I am not rejected, nor will I ever be. I am fully accepted. God tells me he was 'pleased to make me his own.' That's the polar opposition of rejection: it's total acceptance with no qualifications. He was *pleased* to make me his own! Oh, the number of wounds from rejection that promise covers. Christ himself knew rejection. 'He came to that which was his own, but his own did not receive him' (John 1:11). He understands the sting of being turned away by his own people. And yet he didn't despise his rejectors. He still loved them. In the same way, the ones who have rejected me are forgiven by me and accepted by me. And those who have been rejected by others are loved by me. Knowing the pain of rejection, I'm careful not to say or do anything that someone else — particularly a child or loved one — might wrongly perceive as rejection. I keep my heart open to all."

Pray the Promise

Father, no one on this earth has known the depth of rejection you have known. Both in your desire to be a father to all, but also in the person of your Son, Jesus. His model of forgiveness — "Father, forgive them, for they do not know what they are doing" — shows me how you forgive, Lord. Thank you for accepting me — for purposely accepting me. Being accepted by you heals so many of my wounds, Lord. So many.

∽

"The answer to rejection is acceptance. Human acceptance, however, will not heal the damaged emotions after rejection has done its dirty work. It does help, and often it will be the only help available, but the experience of being accepted in Christ is the only true curative."

— CHARLES R. SOLOMON

Repentance from My Sins Frees Me to Move On in Christ

The Truth according to God's Word

Turn from evil and do good;
   then you will dwell in the land forever. (Ps. 37:27)

"Repent, then, and turn to God, so that your sins may be wiped out, that times of refreshing may come from the Lord." (Acts 3:19)

Godly sorrow brings repentance that leads to salvation and leaves no regret, but worldly sorrow brings death. (2 Cor. 7:10)

The Truth

Repentance is a changing of the mind, a turning in the opposite direction. When we turn away from, or repent of, our sin, we simultaneously turn toward something else. That something else is a Someone else. In other words, to turn from sin is to turn toward God. *Repentance is often the very cure we seek to many of our troubles.* Sometimes repentance is the only key to open the lock that imprisons us.

Tell Yourself the Truth

"I have a repentant heart for the many sins in my past. I now hate my sin and turn from it the minute I'm aware of my desire for it. As I turn away from sin, I turn toward God. By facing him, my back is to my sinful desires. I never have a need to do an about-face to return to the sin I have left behind. I keep my eyes on Christ, and my former life, fully repented of, is behind me."

Pray the Promise

Lord, you know I no longer desire my sins. I have repented and turned away from sin and toward you. May my heart be sensitive to temptation to sin, rejecting it the moment it appears in my life.

∽

"Man is born with his face turned away from God. When he truly repents, he is turned right round toward God; he leaves his old life."

—D. L. MOODY

My Trials Won't Defeat Me. I Am **Resilient** in Christ

The Truth according to God's Word

Though the righteous fall seven times, they rise again. (Prov. 24:16)

I know what it is to be in need, and I know what it is to have plenty. I have learned the secret of being content in any and every situation, whether well fed or hungry, whether living in plenty or in want. (Phil. 4:12)

The Truth

We face many potential defeats in life as circumstances and bad decisions take their toll. But in Christ we come back from our failures. Resilience is our heritage. Ask Peter. After his bitter denial of Christ—a travesty that would end the ministries of the most earnest Christians—Peter cried his tears and went on to be used greatly by God. He didn't let his personal defeat become the end of his story. Neither should we. Instead, we must have the determination and resilience to stand up and move ahead.

Tell Yourself the Truth

"I am a survivor. I have had many defeats in my life, but God has brought me back from them all. Yes, I am resilient in Christ. Nothing can take me down and keep me down. I may stumble seven times, but I will rise again each time a stronger person. I don't fear my stumbles; they propel me forward in a way that a person who has never stumbled can't appreciate. I thank God for the resilient spirit he has given me."

Pray the Promise

Praise you, Father, for the resilience you have given me. Though I stumble; you pick me up and dust me off, and I continue on in your love and care. I'm staying on the path, Lord, no matter the potential stumbling blocks ahead. I no longer fear stumbling, as long as you're there.

❧

"At the timberline where the storms strike with the most fury, the sturdiest trees are found."

— HUDSON TAYLOR

I **Rest** in the One Who Called Me to His Light Burden

The Truth according to God's Word

"My Presence will go with you, and I will give you rest." (Ex. 33:14)

Thus says the LORD: "Stand by the roads, and look, and ask for the ancient paths, where the good way is; and walk in it, and find rest for your souls. But they said, 'We will not walk in it.'" (Jer. 6:16 ESV)

"Come to Me, all you who labor and are heavy laden, and I will give you rest. Take My yoke upon you and learn from Me, for I am gentle and lowly in heart, and you will find rest for your souls. For My yoke is easy and My burden is light." (Matt. 11:28–30 NKJV)

There remains, then, a Sabbath-rest for the people of God; for anyone who enters God's rest also rests from their works, just as God did from his. (Heb. 4:9–10)

The Truth

One of the most delightful invitations of all time is this: "Come to Me, all you who labor and are heavy laden, and I will give you rest. Take My yoke upon you and learn from Me, for I am gentle and lowly in heart, and you will find rest for your souls. For My yoke is easy, and My burden is light." I've accepted that invitation to rest. How about you?

Tell Yourself the Truth

"In the past, I worked hard to be pleasing to God. Now I please God by resting fully in Christ. I rest in his finished work on my behalf. I rest in his power, his comfort, his love for me. Never again will I strive for the very things I can have only through true rest in Christ. In his rest, I'm refreshed to do his will. I'm at peace."

Pray the Promise

Lord, you provide rest for the weary—rest from all our works, all our striving, all our day-to-day stresses. When I rest in you, I find complete peace and joy.

∽

"To every toiling, heavy-laden sinner, Jesus says, 'Come to me and rest.' But there are many toiling, heavy-laden believers too. For them this same invitation is meant. Note well the words of Jesus if you are heavy-laden with your service, and do not mistake it. It is not, 'Go, labor on,' as perhaps you imagine. On the contrary, it is stop, turn back, 'Come to me and rest.' Never, never did Christ send a heavy laden one to work; never, never did he send a hungry one, a weary one, a sick or sorrowing one, away on any service. For such the Bible only says, 'Come, come, come.'"

—J. HUDSON TAYLOR

I Serve a God Who Brings **Restoration** to Lives Ruined by Disaster

The Truth according to God's Word

Though you have made me see troubles,
  many and bitter,
  you will restore my life again;
  from the depths of the earth
  you will again bring me up. (Ps. 71:20)

"So I will restore to you the years that the swarming locust has eaten." (Joel 2:25 NKJV)

And the God of all grace, who called you to his eternal glory in Christ, after you have suffered a little while, will himself restore you and make you strong, firm and steadfast. (1 Peter 5:10)

The Truth

Are you a fixer-upper? Most of us are to some degree. And Jesus is the Master Carpenter who specializes in rebuilding fixer-uppers. He's always looking for his next broken life to restore to wholeness. His first project was Peter, after the fisherman's denial of him. That turned out well. So will his restoration of you.

Tell Yourself the Truth

"With Christ, every morning is a new beginning. That which I messed up yesterday is now under reconstruction today. Jesus Christ is the Master Restorer. He takes what the locusts have robbed from me and restores it handily. In him, I'm constantly made new. Perpetually restored, perpetually complete in Christ."

Pray the Promise

God, you know the projects in my life that need restoration, because I am indeed a fixer-upper. Please keep the fresh new mornings coming, full as they are with new mercies from you and a replenishing of what the locusts of life have taken from me.

∽

"Most laws condemn the soul and pronounce sentence. The result of the law of my God is perfect. It condemns but forgives. It restores — more than abundantly — what it takes away."

— JIM ELLIOT

I Live in the Light of the **Return of Christ.** I Will Be Ready

The Truth according to God's Word

"Therefore keep watch, because you do not know on what day your Lord will come." (Matt. 24:42)

"Men of Galilee," they said, "why do you stand here looking into the sky? This same Jesus, who has been taken from you into heaven, will come back in the same way you have seen him go into heaven." (Acts 1:11)

"In just a little while,
    he who is coming will come
    and will not delay." (Heb. 10:37)

Be patient and stand firm, because the Lord's coming is near. (James 5:8)

"Look, I am coming soon! My reward is with me, and I will give to each person according to what they have done. I am the Alpha and the Omega, the First and the Last, the Beginning and the End." (Rev. 22:12 – 13)

The Truth

Can a reasonable person view all the Scriptures about Christ's return (only a few of which are above) and doubt that it will happen just as he promised? Christ *will* return, but no one knows the day or the hour. We don't need to know the time of his return in order to be ready. The beauty of not knowing the date keeps the romance alive, expecting our Lover's return. It's our blessed hope for tomorrow.

Tell Yourself the Truth

"I heed the warnings of Scripture about being ready when Christ returns. I pay no attention to the many scoffers who deny his soon return. They must answer for themselves. My answer is simply to be ready as if he is coming today."

Pray the Promise

Even so, come quickly, Lord Jesus!

∽

"Christ is with us until the world's end. Let his little flock be bold therefore."

— WILLIAM TYNDALE

I Believe in the Lord Jesus Christ. Salvation Is Fully Mine

The Truth according to God's Word

To all who did receive him, to those who believed in his name, he gave the right to become children of God. (John 1:12)

If you confess with your mouth the Lord Jesus and believe in your heart that God has raised Him from the dead, you will be saved. For with the heart one believes unto righteousness, and with the mouth confession is made unto salvation. (Rom. 10:9–10 NKJV)

"Everyone who calls on the name of the Lord will be saved." (Rom. 10:13)

The Truth

Salvation—saving people from destruction—is God's designed plan. He knew all along that we would need a Redeemer. And because God designed the plan of salvation, it's a foolproof plan that cannot be in any way dismantled, changed, rearranged, or canceled. According to this wonderfully designed plan, *all* who will believe and trust in Christ must be saved. If you have trusted in Christ, you are saved and will not be lost.

Never trust your feelings as a barometer of your salvation. Feelings do not save us; only faith in Christ saves us. Always remember that being a Christian is a miraculous thing. Being born again from above? Living daily in the power of God's Holy Spirit? Praying to a listening God who invites us to come to him? How are these things not miracles? We must remind ourselves daily of our great salvation.

Rejoice in your status as a child of God. Thank him daily for his consuming love for you evidenced by the fact that he saved you and that in so doing, it was his work and not your own.

Tell Yourself the Truth

"Because I do believe in Jesus Christ—and that he died for my sins—I have eternal life. I acknowledge that my future as a Christian is assured because of my faith in Christ. I am now a possessor of the eternal life God so freely gives everyone who believes in Christ. Because that life is eternal, it will not be lost. Yes, I am saved to the uttermost. *It is finished.*"

Pray the Promise

Lord, I know that my salvation is wholly your work on my behalf. I know only too well that I don't deserve this gift, but I believe it is mine because of Christ's death on the cross for my sins. Thank you, Lord, for this amazing gift!

∽

"It is our privilege to know that we are saved."

—D. L. MOODY

I Overcome Every **Satanic Attack** through Christ

The Truth according to God's Word

"My prayer is not that you take them out of the world but that you protect them from the evil one." (John 17:15)

Do not give the devil a foothold. (Eph. 4:27)

Put on the full armor of God, so that you can take your stand against the devil's schemes. (Eph. 6:11)

In addition to all this, take up the shield of faith, with which you can extinguish all the flaming arrows of the evil one. (Eph. 6:16)

Submit yourselves, then, to God. Resist the devil, and he will flee from you. (James 4:7)

Be alert and of sober mind. Your enemy the devil prowls around like a roaring lion looking for someone to devour. (1 Peter 5:8)

The Truth

Satan is still active on this earth, seeking whom he may devour by feeding them lies about themselves and God. He knows you were meant for great things and wants to stop them from happening. Recognizing Satan's lies and standing against his attacks makes us stronger and enables us to live out God's plan for us. We are invincible to any satanic assault as we put on the full armor of God.

Tell Yourself the Truth

"I have no fear of Satan. He is defeated and God has given me the promises I need to withstand his temptations. Though he tries to lure me with deceit, pride, and lies about my worth, I recognize his tactics and denounce them for what they are. God's truth overcomes Satan's lies every time. To defeat Satan's attacks on me, I do the following:

1. Stay alert and of sober mind.
2. Resist sinful temptations.
3. Submit myself to God and resist the devil.
4. Put on the armor of God (see Eph. 6).
5. Don't give the enemy a foothold through anger.
6. Stand firmly on the Word of God.
7. Walk in the power of the Holy Spirit."

Pray the Promise

Lord God, thank you that the "full armor" I wear ensures my complete victory over Satan's attacks. I stand firm in my life in Christ and watch him destroy the works and ways of the devil.

∽

"The triumphant Christian does not fight for victory; he celebrates a victory already won."

— REGINALD WALLIS

My **Self-Esteem** Is Based on Christ's Love for Me

The Truth according to God's Word

So God created mankind in his own image,
in the image of God he created them;
male and female he created them. (Gen. 1:27)

Keep me as the apple of Your eye;
Hide me under the shadow of Your wings. (Ps. 17:8 NKJV)

For you created my inmost being; you knit me together in my mother's womb. I praise you because I am fearfully and wonderfully made; your works are wonderful, I know that full well. (Ps. 139:13–14)

"The LORD your God is with you,
the Mighty Warrior who saves.
He will take great delight in you;
in his love he will no longer rebuke you,
but will rejoice over you with singing." (Zeph. 3:17)

"Are not two sparrows sold for a penny? Yet not one of them will fall to the ground outside your Father's care. And even the very hairs of your head are all numbered. So don't be afraid; you are worth more than many sparrows." (Matt. 10:29–31)

We are God's handiwork, created in Christ Jesus to do good works, which God prepared in advance for us to do. (Eph. 2:10)

The Truth

Our esteem, confidence, and identity flow from the fact that we were created to bear God's image. We are like him in that respect. We are the pinnacle of God's creation on earth. We are not random collections of cells, flesh, and bones. Our spirit bears witness to the fact that we come from God and that we were created for his glory. Blessed are the Christians who settle into their new identity as a unique creation of God.

Tell Yourself the Truth

"I am God's handiwork, made in his image to do great things. I have the traits of my heavenly Father imprinted on my spirit. I have the power to love, bring healing, tell the Good News, and create beautiful things, and in so doing, proclaim the glory of God. My Heavenly Father delights in me and rejoices over me with singing. He made me to be an object of his love. Because I am special to God, I have no doubt as to my true worth. I can love myself because God loves me."

Pray the Promise

Dear Father, how can I thank you for loving me? First there was your love in knitting me together in my mother's womb. Then your love followed me all the days until I met you. Then, even during my stubborn episodes, you stuck with me. You knew there was something in me of value. In fact, value equal to the life of your Son. Lord, thank you for who I am. It would be an insult to you for me to wish I was someone else, so I thank you for me, this piece of clay you've invested with your life and love.

⤸

A missionary lady's emotional problems had had a negative impact on her ministry and that of her husband. They had left the field after almost twenty years, and she came for help. In eliciting the history, the spiritual counselor had learned that as the woman was growing up, her father had told her she was not worth her salt, so of course, that is the way she felt. The counselor told her, "Your earthly father says that you are not worth your salt; your heavenly Father says you are worth his Son. Now which will be the basis for your identity from this point on — salt or Son?"

— CHARLES R. SOLOMON

Serving Is the True Mark of a Christ Follower

The Truth according to God's Word

"The greatest among you will be your servant." (Matt. 23:11)

Sitting down, Jesus called the Twelve and said, "Anyone who wants to be first must be the very last, and the servant of all." (Mark 9:35)

You, my brothers and sisters, were called to be free. But do not use your freedom to indulge the flesh; rather, serve one another humbly in love. For the entire law is fulfilled in keeping this one command: "Love your neighbor as yourself." (Gal. 5:13 – 14)

Each of you should use whatever gift you have received to serve others, as faithful stewards of God's grace in its various forms. (1 Peter 4:10)

The Truth

If we really want to be like Jesus, we will serve others. That's what he came to do and taught us to do. To serve others is to serve Christ.

Tell Yourself the Truth

"There is healing power in servanthood because it gets my mind off of myself and onto the needs of others. Serving is giving the gift of myself to others. God leads me to places of service where I can bring joy to the joyless, happiness to the unhappy, or tangible help to those in need. I find my place in the body of Christ as that of a servant. The more I serve, the more I reflect Christ who came in the role of a servant. I love to walk in his footsteps."

Pray the Promise

Thank you Lord for eyes open to the needs of others, ears open to their cries, and feet that will take me across their paths. Teach me to serve, not to be served.

⌒

"Lord Jesus, I offer myself for your people. In any way. Any time."

— CORRIE TEN BOOM

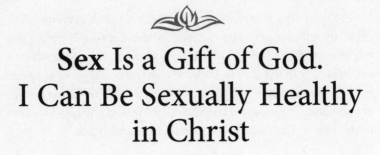

Sex Is a Gift of God. I Can Be Sexually Healthy in Christ

The Truth according to God's Word

You are to abstain from ... sexual immorality. (Acts 15:29)

Let us behave decently, as in the daytime, not in carousing and drunkenness, not in sexual immorality and debauchery. (Rom. 13:13)

Flee from sexual immorality. All other sins a person commits are outside the body, but whoever sins sexually, sins against their own body. (1 Cor. 6:18)

We should not commit sexual immorality. (1 Cor. 10:8)

But among you there must not be even a hint of sexual immorality. (Eph. 5:3)

It is God's will that you should ... avoid sexual immorality. (1 Thess. 4:3)

The Truth

Sex, as invented by God, is to be treasured and enjoyed by two people whom God has joined together. Today sex in many modern cultures has been corrupted from God's original design. Many people, including some Christians, are caught up in the pursuit of sexual pleasure, driven by lust, only to discover that it's a drug that never satisfies. However, *God's design for sexual expression* never fails to deliver. Sexually healthy Christians who are married not only enjoy sanctified sex, but they reject the world's unhealthy sexual aberrations, including casual sexual encounters, pornography, adultery, lust, premarital sex, and any other forms of sexual license that robs people of God's designed pleasure in sex.

Tell Yourself the Truth

"God's Word is clear: sexual immorality is to be avoided at all costs. I respect the gift of sex and know that sexual desire is something ordained by God. However, due to my fallen nature, I am tempted. Nevertheless I will not engage in unhealthy and sinful sexual activities that diminish the awe of God's design for sex. I will instead respect God's boundaries for sexual activity. I will not pursue sexual encounters beyond those with my life mate. [If single:] I will keep my sexual desires in check if and until God brings a life mate into my life. I reject the unhealthy sexuality the world chases after — only to their disappointment. Healthy sex is a benefit of following Christ and his way, and I desire to live a sexually whole and healthy life."

Pray the Promise

Lord, is there anything you invented that has caused more trouble for humankind than the corruption of sexual desire? So many lives are ruined by it. Mine will not be one of them. God, I will trust you for the fulfillment of my sexual desires. I will not act out sexually beyond the bounds of married life. I will be loyal to the mate you give me. I will not allow pornography or other corruptions of sexuality to mess up my life. Father, use my sexuality to bring honor to you.

❧

"The reproduction of mankind is a great marvel and mystery. Had God consulted me in the matter, I should have advised him to continue the generation of the species by fashioning them out of clay."

— Martin Luther

Sin Is My Enemy, but I Can Overcome Sin through Christ

The Truth according to God's Word

O God, You know my foolishness;
 And my sins are not hidden from You. (Ps. 69:5 NKJV)

Whoever conceals their sins does not prosper,
 but the one who confesses and renounces them finds mercy.
 (Prov. 28:13)

Let the wicked forsake their ways
 and the unrighteous their thoughts.
 Let them turn to the LORD, and he will have mercy on them,
 and to our God, for he will freely pardon. (Isa. 55:7)

For all have sinned and fall short of the glory of God. (Rom. 3:23)

Sin shall no longer be your master, because you are not under the law, but under grace. (Rom. 6:14).

Since we are surrounded by such a great cloud of witnesses, let us throw off everything that hinders and the sin that so easily entangles. And let us run with perseverance the race marked out for us. (Heb. 12:1)

The Truth

Sin is that which separates people from God. The solution for sin is Jesus Christ. He is the *only* solution to sin, but he is enough. Sin must be dealt with early. Unchecked sin gains momentum and can eventually consume a life. When allowed to grow to full term, sin wins and a life is destroyed.

Tell Yourself the Truth

"Sin is a heavy weight to bear. Thank God, it is not my weight to bear, but Christ bore it for me. The sin problem in my life was fully dealt with on the cross. When he was crucified and died, so did my sinful self die. In his resurrection, I too rose to new life. What then can sin do to me now? *Nothing.* Sin shall not be my master, for I am not under law but under grace."

Pray the Promise

Thank you, Father, for Jesus, my sin-bearer. I'm free from the penalty and power from all my sin. By the power of your Spirit, I now live a sin-resistant life, because sin is no longer my master. Thank you, Father, for the grace that empowers me to live victoriously. What good news!

〜

"Either sin is with you, lying on your shoulders, or it is lying on Christ, the Lamb of God. Now if it is lying on your back, you are lost; but if it is resting on Christ, you are free, and you will be saved. Now choose what you want."

— MARTIN LUTHER

God Eases My Every **Sorrow** with His Compassion

The Truth according to God's Word

Weeping may endure for a night,
    But joy comes in the morning. (Ps. 30:5 NKJV)

Be merciful to me, LORD, for I am in distress;
    my eyes grow weak with sorrow,
    my soul and body with grief. (Ps. 31:9)

My soul is weary with sorrow;
    strengthen me according to your word. (Ps. 119:28)

You who are my Comforter in sorrow,
    my heart is faint within me. (Jer. 8:18)

The Truth

Christ, the man of sorrows, suffered deeply. Sometimes so must we. But like Christ, our sorrow lasts only for a season and then gives way to joy. While we suffer, God is always there for us as our Comforter and caregiver.

Tell Yourself the Truth

"When I sorrow, I add patience to my sorrow, knowing that this is just a season and I will soon enter into a new season. Meanwhile, God is with me, holding me up, keeping me walking step-by-step in the right direction. I know that just as Jesus cried at the news of Lazarus's death, so too he sorrows with me as I grieve. All sorrow is eventually beneficial, if for no other reason than that it teaches me compassion for others who sorrow. I will offer them comfort as they grieve."

Pray the Promise

Lord, my sorrow is deep. But your compassion and comfort are deeper still. Thank you for your care and love. Keep me through this season, and teach me how to comfort others in their sorrow.

∽

"Every tear of sorrow sown by the righteous springs up a pearl."

— MATTHEW HENRY

God Is **Sovereign**. He Is in Control of What Enters My Life

The Truth according to God's Word

"Lord, the God of our ancestors, are you not the God who is in heaven? You rule over all the kingdoms of the nations. Power and might are in your hand, and no one can withstand you." (2 Chron. 20:6)

"I know that you can do all things; no purpose of yours can be thwarted." (Job 42:2)

Our God is in heaven;
    he does whatever pleases him. (Ps. 115:3)

The Lord will perfect that which concerns me. (Ps. 138:8 NKJV)

"With God all things are possible." (Matt. 19:26)

The Truth

God is in charge of his universe. That he desires to use our prayers to accomplish his will is breathtaking. Without our assurance of

God's sovereignty, our prayers would be weak. How could we count on a God who isn't sovereign to offer us help in time of need? Our great strength in prayer, then, is not dependent so much on us as it is dependent on our God who, because of his sovereignty, is able to answer our prayers.

Tell Yourself the Truth

"I serve a sovereign God. In prayer I lay hold of Jesus' words that 'with God, all things are possible'—possible because God is the Master of all, with the ability to reach down into my world and move me forward in my life, often in unexpected and even curious ways. And yet the result of trusting an all-powerful, in-charge God is knowing that he will 'perfect that which concerns me.'"

Pray the Promise

Father God, you are a good God and you are a sovereign God. Sometimes it's hard, but I will trust all that you do even when I don't understand it. I pray that in your sovereignty you will work on my behalf so that nothing will impede my destiny. I will finish the race you set before me, Lord.

∽

"Divine sovereignty is not the sovereignty of a tyrannical despot, but the exercised pleasure of one who is infinitely wise and good! Because God is infinitely wise, he cannot err, and because he is infinitely righteous, he will not do wrong. Here then is the preciousness of this truth. The mere fact itself that God's will is irresistible and irreversible fills me with fear, but once I realize that God wills only that which is good, my heart is made to rejoice."

— ARTHUR W. PINK

When Faced with **Spiritual Warfare**, I Overcome the Enemy Every Time

The Truth according to God's Word

For our struggle is not against flesh and blood, but against the rulers, against the authorities, against the powers of this dark world and against the spiritual forces of evil in the heavenly realms. (Eph. 6:12)

And having disarmed the powers and authorities, he made a public spectacle of them, triumphing over them by the cross. (Col. 2:15)

Submit yourselves, then, to God. Resist the devil, and he will flee from you. (James 4:7)

You, dear children, are from God and have overcome them, because the one who is in you is greater than the one who is in the world. (1 John 4:4)

The Truth

Although Satan has been defeated, sometimes we must remind him (and perhaps ourselves) that he has no power or influence in our lives. The results of not taking such a stand can be disastrous. Give Satan an inch and he takes a mile.

Tell Yourself the Truth

"My struggle is not against flesh and blood. My war is with the powers of darkness and the spiritual forces of evil in the heavenly realms. I war against them with great success by constantly reminding them and myself of Christ's victory at Calvary. I boldly inform the enemy that he has no authority in my life. His efforts to derail my life cannot succeed. I never allow Satan any foothold in my life but react at once against his strategies."

Pray the Promise

Father, I know I have authority over the enemy when he initiates a spiritual attack. I thank you that you have not left your people defenseless against his tactics. Thank you that you both protect me and give me strength and power. I overcome Satan through Christ. Praise you, Lord!

∽

"A Christian life is an unending engagement on the battlefield."

— WATCHMAN NEE

My **Steps** Are Ordered of the Lord. I Cannot Fail

The Truth according to God's Word

The steps of a good man are ordered by the LORD,
   And He delights in his way. (Ps. 37:23 NKJV)

When you walk, your steps will not be hampered;
   when you run, you will not stumble. (Prov. 4:12)

In their hearts humans plan their course,
   but the LORD establishes their steps. (Prov. 16:9)

A person's steps are directed by the LORD.
   How then can anyone understand their own way? (Prov. 20:24)

LORD, I know that people's lives are not their own;
   it is not for them to direct their steps. (Jer. 10:23)

The Truth

On an uncertain path, we walk carefully lest we trip. But on God's certain path, with his Word as our lantern, our steps are secure, having been ordered by the Lord. Though the lantern shows us only the next few feet of our journey, we can walk confidently ahead, the light of his Word continually ahead of us. Though we don't know where the journey will take us, we do know that at the end of our path, Jesus stands waiting. We simply need to keep walking, and we'll get there.

Tell Yourself the Truth

"God delights in my way; therefore my steps are confident, firmly on the path, for I know who is just ahead of me, blazing my trail. My steps are headed in a good direction—the perfect will of God for me. I do not look at the walk of others with envy. God has a unique design for my life, and I will arrive at my God-ordained destination when my last footstep on earth is taken."

Pray the Promise

Step-by-step, Lord, I follow you. Keep my path straight, my feet firmly planted, my lantern shining brightly, and my eyes on the finish line. With that assurance, I will one day find Jesus waiting at the end of my road. Lord, I pray I may hear you say, "Well done, good and faithful servant."

$\backsim$

"We are too apt to look and see how others walk, which is not faith, and to allow our own steps to be more or less affected by the walk of others around us. But in so doing, my soul is not carrying out the spirit of life in my walk."

—G. V. WIGRAM

I Release My Stress to the Lord, and He Brings Peace

The Truth according to God's Word

"Do not worry about tomorrow, for tomorrow will worry about itself. Each day has enough trouble of its own." (Matt. 6:34)

As Jesus and his disciples were on their way, he came to a village where a woman named Martha opened her home to him. She had a sister called Mary, who sat at the Lord's feet listening to what he said. But Martha was distracted by all the preparations that had to be made. She came to him and asked, "Lord, don't you care that my sister has left me to do the work by myself? Tell her to help me!"

"Martha, Martha," the Lord answered, "you are worried and upset about many things, but few things are needed—or indeed only one. Mary has chosen what is better, and it will not be taken away from her." (Luke 10:38–42)

"Who of you by worrying can add a single hour to your life? Since you cannot do this very little thing, why do you worry about the rest?" (Luke 12:25–26)

The Truth

Every generation has its unique stresses. Ours may be different than the ones our grandparents faced, but our God has not changed. He watched over them in their stresses, and his eyes are on us in our stressful situations. Knowing this, we should consider that every stress is either a signal that we're relying on our own strength or that we're taking on responsibilities God never meant us to have.

Tell Yourself the Truth

"God's presence goes with me wherever I go, whatever stressful situation I face. Therefore I will not worry. God is willing to take my stress, so why should I keep it for myself? He sees, he hears, he feels all that I feel. Nothing stressing me escapes his attention. He is the divine filter through which everything must pass that comes to me. He has the remedy for every stress in my life—and that remedy is to *rest* in him or to abandon some responsibilities he never meant me to have."

Pray the Promise

My life, Lord, is often stressful. You know the reasons, the people, the events, the time crunches, the workload, the money issues, the health issues, the family issues—you know them all Lord. Take them, Father. Take this stress, and in return, give me your peace.

∽

"God knows what each one of us is dealing with. He knows our pressures. He knows our conflicts. And He has made a provision for each and every one of them. That provision is Himself in the person of the Holy Spirit, indwelling us and empowering us to respond rightly."

—KAY ARTHUR

God Will Tear Down the **Strongholds** That Keep Me Imprisoned

The Truth according to God's Word

One who is wise can go up against the city of the mighty
and pull down the stronghold in which they trust. (Prov. 21:22)

For though we live in the world, we do not wage war as the world does. The weapons we fight with are not the weapons of the world. On the contrary, they have divine power to demolish strongholds. (2 Cor. 10:3–4)

The Truth

Strongholds of the enemy are meant to be torn down. They exist as areas of our lives where we have given the enemy temporary access. Unless we demolish those strongholds, they become stronger and we become weaker against them. But God has given even the least of us the power to overcome our strongholds. Some strongholds take longer than others to overcome, but we mustn't lose heart. We must keep standing strong in faith against every stronghold the enemy tries to establish in us. We must be free to live.

Tell Yourself the Truth

"Spiritual strongholds don't spring up overnight. They result from one deviant thought taking root in my mind, and from there Satan has his foot in the door. I resist strongholds at the very onset. I will not give Satan the opportunity to build a fortress from an evil thought. Strongholds from my past are broken by bringing the full force of Christ's victory into my life. Everything that could be done to free me was done on the cross. I now have the authority to claim that victory in my own life. Strongholds are always based on a lie. I bring the truth to bear on the stronghold, and it must go even if I must enforce the victory over the course of several days or weeks. I will not be under the burden of any of Satan's strongholds. I am free in Christ, and I mean to resist every tactic of the enemy that would try to keep me in chains. Freedom from all strongholds is *mine*."

Pray the Promise

Father, your intention is that every child of yours be free from the strongholds that keep us captive. To that end, I crush each of the enemy's strongholds in my life. I take back every inch of ground he has stolen from me. Thank you, Lord, for the authority you've given me in your name to rout Satan and tear down his strongholds. Thank you that I am stronger than my spiritual enemies.

∾

"Spiritual strongholds begin with a thought. One thought becomes a consideration. A consideration develops into an attitude, which leads then to action. Action repeated becomes a habit, and a habit establishes a 'power base for the enemy,' that is, a stronghold."

—ELISABETH ELLIOT

Suffering Happens. I Will Trust God to Give Me Grace and Patience, for I Know It Will Pass

The Truth according to God's Word

My comfort in my suffering is this:
   Your promise preserves my life. (Ps. 119:50)

Now if we are children, then we are heirs—heirs of God and co-heirs with Christ, if indeed we share in his sufferings in order that we may also share in his glory. I consider that our present sufferings are not worth comparing with the glory that will be revealed in us. (Rom. 8:17–18)

And the God of all grace, who called you to his eternal glory in Christ, after you have suffered a little while, will himself restore you and make you strong, firm and steadfast. (1 Peter 5:10)

The Truth

Suffering is never pleasant. But when we suffer, we can look for something meaningful to come from it. For example, when we suffer, we learn compassion for others. We see Jesus more clearly as we fathom his willingness to suffer for our guilt, though he was innocent. Why? Because he looked beyond the time of suffering and saw the end result. There was hidden value in his suffering. Might there also be in ours?

Tell Yourself the Truth

"I don't choose suffering in my life, but sometimes suffering happens. When it does, I wait prayerfully, learning all I can from it. I especially try to imagine how I would help another person going through what I'm going through. I do not waste my suffering."

Pray the Promise

Lord, release me soon from my suffering. I have learned much, but I am weary. Thank you for your promise that you will restore me after this suffering. I will take this experience and use it to encourage others. This time has not been wasted, dear Father; but now I need for this trial to be lifted from me.

⁓

"O child of suffering, be thou patient; God has not passed thee over in his providence. He who is the feeder of sparrows will also furnish you with what you need. Sit not down in despair; hope on, hope ever. Take up the arms of faith against a sea of trouble, and your opposition shall yet end your distresses. There is One who careth for you."

— CHARLES SPURGEON

To **Surrender** Is to Allow God to Direct My Life

The Truth according to God's Word

My son, give me your heart
   and let your eyes delight in my ways. (Prov. 23:26)

"Come to me, all you who are weary and burdened, and I will give you rest. Take my yoke upon you and learn from me, for I am gentle and humble in heart, and you will find rest for your souls. For my yoke is easy and my burden is light." (Matt. 11:28–30)

Submit yourselves, then, to God. (James 4:7)

The Truth

Surrender to God is empowering. It's an act of absolute submission to God, nothing held back. It is freedom to be God's perfect *us*. Likewise, to refuse to surrender to God robs us of God's best for us. And it diminishes our power to live the abundant life, for abundance comes only through absolute surrender.

Tell Yourself the Truth

"God takes great pleasure in receiving what I surrender to him. My part is surrender, and God's part is receiving. And yet I so often doubt that he will receive what I surrender—whether it be my burdens, health, children, or finances—and so my surrender is weak. But if I could see the great delight with which God welcomes my surrendered burdens, I would hold nothing back from him. *Just so, I hold nothing back now."*

Pray the Promise

Lord, I give up all things to you. Show me the joy of surrender. Remind me, too, of the disastrous results of not living a surrendered life. By faith, Lord, I hold nothing back. I'm yours entirely.

༄

"Let God have your life; he can do more with it than you can."

—D. L. MOODY

My **Temptations** Are Not Unique. Everyone Faces Temptation, but I Can Stand Strong and Prevail

The Truth according to God's Word

No temptation has overtaken you except such as is common to man; but God is faithful, who will not allow you to be tempted beyond what you are able, but with the temptation will also make the way of escape, that you may be able to bear it. (1 Cor. 10:13 NKJV)

When tempted, no one should say, "God is tempting me." For God cannot be tempted by evil, nor does he tempt anyone; but each person is tempted when they are dragged away by their own evil desire and enticed. Then, after desire has conceived, it gives birth to sin; and sin, when it is full-grown, gives birth to death (James 1:13–15)

The Truth

Everyone faces temptation. *Everyone.* But not all who are tempted give in to its magnetic pull. Some stand strong. Some overcome—

and so can you. You do not have to yield to the compulsions that feed on your natural weaknesses. You *can* find the way of escape that God provides. Remember, it's never God who is your tempter. In truth, we are tempted by our own evil desires. God is not the source of our temptation; he is the solace in our temptation.

Tell Yourself the Truth

"My temptations are not unique. Others are facing the very same temptations I do. Even Jesus was tempted. But God is faithful and has given me a way of escape. He knows the limits I can handle and will never allow my temptations to exceed those limits. I can bear my temptations by taking every way of escape God provides. In times past, temptation has come at me so quickly I've not taken time to watch for my God-appointed way of escape. But now I look for and recognize how to escape the snare of temptation. I lean hard on God, and I rejoice in him who has made me an overcomer in every circumstance—including temptation. I now see every temptation as a fresh challenge to God's strength in me. His supernatural power in me is stronger than every temptation that assails me."

Pray the Promise

Father, I don't like my temptations. They lure me into doing things I don't want to do—as you well know. As I stand on your Word against my temptations, I trust your promises to do their work. I will expect and watch for ways of escape from every temptation, and I know I will not experience any temptation I can't bear. When temptations come, Lord, I won't resist in my own natural strength (indeed I can't) but will rely on walking in your Spirit to bring me through.

"My temptations have been my Masters in Divinity."

— MARTIN LUTHER

I Have Much to Be Thankful For. I Overflow with Gratitude and **Thanksgiving** to God

The Truth according to God's Word

Give thanks to the LORD, for he is good; his love endures forever. (1 Chron. 16:34)

I will praise God's name in song
  and glorify him with thanksgiving. (Ps. 69:30)

Give thanks in all circumstances; for this is God's will for you in Christ Jesus. (1 Thess. 5:18)

The Truth

We are often too busy to remember where we've come from and who has brought us this far. Take a thanksgiving break every so often during the day and breathe a prayer of gratitude. Be thankful in *all* circumstances.

Tell Yourself the Truth

"I have much to be thankful for, even though I'm often slow to say it. I *do* know better than anyone else all the things I have to thank God for. May God be praised for it all."

Pray the Promise

Lord, every day in my life is Thanksgiving Day. My heart overflows with gratitude for all you've given me, for what you're doing in my life, for the fact that I'm still here living out the life you planned for me. Thank you, thank you, thank you.

⤳

"Thanksgiving will draw our hearts out to God and keep us engaged with Him; it will take our attention from ourselves and give the Spirit room in our hearts."

— Andrew Murray

God Has Allotted Enough Time for Everything in My Life. I Will Not Stress

The Truth according to God's Word

Show me, LORD, my life's end
    and the number of my days;
    let me know how fleeting my life is.
    You have made my days a mere handbreadth;
    the span of my years is as nothing before you.
    Everyone is but a breath. (Ps. 39:4–5)

Teach us to number our days,
    that we may gain a heart of wisdom. (Ps. 90:12)

Be very careful, then, how you live—not as unwise but as wise, making the most of every opportunity, because the days are evil. (Eph. 5:15–16)

The Truth

Our times are in God's hands, not ours. We have time in our lives for everything God calls us to. Let's not waste it on what he has not called us to.

Tell Yourself the Truth

"God numbers my days, and I'm a good steward of each and every one. I don't stress over time. Time is my friend, not my enemy. I treat every day as a fresh gift from God, ready to be lived to the fullest loving him. I honor God with my time, and he seems to miraculously expand it for me. I get more done when I entrust my time to him. Though I sometimes feel rushed, I know there is exactly enough time left in my life to accomplish all of God's plans for me. I do not 'kill time.' I *redeem* time."

Pray the Promise

Each minute, Lord, is a precious gift from you. Help me to be sensitive to time. Help me to know when to work and when to stop and rest. Help me find the time wasters in my life and remove them. You, O Lord, are the keeper of my days. Keep them well for me.

⤳

"Time is given us to use in view of eternity."

— Harry Ironside

My **Tongue** Is a Fountain of Blessing to Others

The Truth according to God's Word

"As long as I have life within me,
    the breath of God in my nostrils,
    my lips will not say anything wicked,
    and my tongue will not utter lies." (Job 27:3–5)

My mouth will tell of your righteous deeds,
    of your saving acts all day long—
    though I know not how to relate them all. (Ps. 71:15)

Set a guard over my mouth, LORD; keep watch over the door of my lips. (Ps. 141:3)

"A good man out of the good treasure of his heart brings forth good; and an evil man out of the evil treasure of his heart brings forth evil. For out of the abundance of the heart his mouth speaks." (Luke 6:45 NKJV)

Do not let any unwholesome talk come out of your mouths, but only what is helpful for building others up according to their needs, that it may benefit those who listen. (Eph. 4:29)

Those who consider themselves religious and yet do not keep a tight rein on their tongues deceive themselves, and their religion is worthless. (James 1:26)

The Truth

Our tongues are instruments of either good or bad. They can either build up or tear down. God designed them for the former purpose. Perhaps that's why there are so many verses in the Bible about the use of our tongue. God knows how valuable it can be when we speak healing words to the hurting. He also knows how easily an undisciplined tongue can inflict wounds. We *must* rein in our unwieldy tongues, and we can do it with his help and power.

Tell Yourself the Truth

"Out of the abundance of my heart, my tongue speaks. I will cultivate my heart with God's Word and good thoughts, and my tongue will share positive, encouraging, edifying words. I will keep my tongue from gossip, lying, swearing, or other destructive talk. My tongue is a fountain of life to those to whom I speak. Healing words come from my mouth. Hurtful words are as poison to my lips. My tongue delights in praising God for his goodness to me. My tongue, like the rest of my body, is fully God's, fully sanctified."

Pray the Promise

Father, may my tongue be a healer, not a wounder. Set a guard over my lips to keep me from using harmful words. Use my tongue to offer praises to you and prayers and encouragement for those who need your help.

⌒

"Beloved, has God sanctified your tongue? Are you willing that he should? Will you give to him the reins of this member, and, henceforth, relinquish to him the right to hold it in suppression, to keep it from idle, evil, false or foolish speech, and use it wholly as the instrument of his will and service?"

— A. B. SIMPSON

When **Tragedy** Happens, I Won't Become Bitter; I Look to God to Bring His Good Result

The Truth according to God's Word

God is our refuge and strength,
    an ever-present help in trouble.
    Therefore we will not fear, though the earth give way
    and the mountains fall into the heart of the sea,
    though its waters roar and foam
    and the mountains quake with their surging. (Ps. 46:1–3)

Have no fear of sudden disaster
    or of the ruin that overtakes the wicked,
    for the LORD will be at your side
    and will keep your foot from being snared. (Prov. 3:25–26)

"In this world you will have trouble. But take heart! I have overcome the world." (John 16:33)

The Truth

God is with us to watch over us in all situations, even tragedies. His being *with* us is the most powerful and comforting thing we could imagine. His presence will be with us through the most difficult times in our lives reassuring us of his care, protection, and never-ending love.

Tell Yourself the Truth

"No one escapes life without facing some sort of tragedy, and often several tragic events. Job wondered at the tragedies in his life but refused to blame God. For his response, Job's later years were more prosperous than his earlier years. And so it is with me. During tragedy, I may have to beat down the temptation to become depressed. I may have to fight to keep my eyes on the future. God will bring me through to a better future, though. He always does."

Pray the Promise

O Lord, tragedy brings many, many tears. Help me see my way through this earthquake in my life. Bring me through by your strength, for otherwise, I'll never make it. As difficult as it is, I will speak faith in the midst of this horror. I will believe you have not deserted me, but you're right here, right now. Walk me step-by-step through to the other side of this dark tunnel. Bring healing to my heart soon.

⌐

"When a train goes through a tunnel and it gets dark, you don't throw away the ticket and jump off. You sit still and trust the engineer."

— CORRIE TEN BOOM

My **Trials** Are God-Given Opportunities for Him to Prove, Once Again, His Faithfulness

The Truth according to God's Word

Consider it pure joy, my brothers and sisters, whenever you face trials of many kinds, because you know that the testing of your faith produces perseverance. (James 1:2–3)

Blessed is the one who perseveres under trial because, having stood the test, that person will receive the crown of life that the Lord has promised to those who love him. (James 1:12)

In all this you greatly rejoice, though now for a little while you may have had to suffer grief in all kinds of trials. (1 Peter 1:6)

The Lord knows how to rescue the godly from trials and to hold the unrighteous for punishment on the day of judgment. (2 Peter 2:9)

The Truth

We will never escape trials in this life, but we can receive the great power that accompanies every trial. For trials reveal our weak faith, our dependence on ourselves, and often our overattachment to this world. When thus revealed, we become aware of God's sufficiency—and God's power to get us through our trials. We can be secure throughout the trial that God watches over us to keep us from falling.

Tell Yourself the Truth

"I am determined to believe that *every* trial that comes my way has God's purposes behind it. When I face a trial, I see that God has a larger purpose waiting for me at the end. I then walk straight ahead toward that purpose. The trial becomes only a pathway to being where God wants me. Though trials are inherently uncomfortable, I know each one is meant to accomplish something important in me and for me. God doesn't permit trials that waste my time and energy. Nor does he enjoy seeing me struggle in pain. Every trial is a package to be unwrapped so that I can discover the goodness God means for me to find."

Pray the Promise

Lord, use this trial to make me strong. That's the only possible benefit I can see from it. I will praise you throughout the ordeal, walking by faith but surely not by sight. Hold me, Lord.

~

"In one thousand trials, it is not five hundred of them that work for the believer's good, but nine hundred and ninety-nine of them, and one beside."

—GEORGE MUELLER

Unanswered Prayer
Is an Oxymoron

The Truth according to God's Word

"Therefore I tell you, whatever you ask for in prayer, believe that you have received it, and it will be yours." (Mark 11:24)

When you ask, you do not receive, because you ask with wrong motives, that you may spend what you get on your pleasures. (James 4:3)

For the eyes of the Lord are on the righteous
    and his ears are attentive to their prayer. (1 Peter 3:12)

This is the confidence we have in approaching God: that if we ask anything according to his will, he hears us. (1 John 5:14)

The Truth

There is no such thing as an unanswered prayer. Every prayer is answered. Sometimes God says yes; but when the answer is no, there is the additional promise, also given to the apostle Paul, that God's grace is sufficient. If you don't see the answer to something you've prayed for, keep praying until you do have an answer. Don't give up.

Tell Yourself the Truth

"Like a child whispering into the ear of his father, I know my heavenly Father hears my every prayer. He hears every sigh, every tear, every cry of agony. He listens intently and knows the answer he will give even before I ask. And that answer is always his will and always his best for me. My prayers, his Word, and his will all work together to bring about his desired end: his perfect will."

Pray the Promise

My prayers, Lord, are to be in perfect alignment with your will. I will try to discern your will in a matter before I pray. May my will be more and more a reflection of your will. May such prayers have an eternal effect in bringing about your desired end in me and in my life.

⌣

"When we pray 'in the Name of Jesus' the answers are in accordance with his nature, and if we think our prayers are unanswered it is because we are not interpreting the answer along this line."

— OSWALD CHAMBERS

All Christians Are Brothers and Sisters and Are to Walk in **Unity**

The Truth according to God's Word

How good and pleasant it is
  when God's people live together in unity! (Ps. 133:1)

I appeal to you, brothers and sisters, in the name of our Lord Jesus Christ, that all of you agree with one another in what you say and that there be no divisions among you, but that you be perfectly united in mind and thought. (1 Cor. 1:10)

Make every effort to keep the unity of the Spirit through the bond of peace. (Eph. 4:3)

Make my joy complete by being like-minded, having the same love, being one in spirit and of one mind. (Phil. 2:2)

Finally, all of you be of one mind, having compassion for one another; love as brothers, be tenderhearted, be courteous. (1 Peter 3:8 NKJV)

The Truth

One of Jesus' final prayers was that we all be "one." I believe God answered that prayer. All true believers are one in him. We all just need to act like it. Nowhere in the Bible is Christ's body, the church, revealed as anything other than *one* body. There are not two, three, four, or more of his body. *Only one.* His church. Though we may vary slightly on some doctrines or worship a bit differently, if we are indeed part of his body, we are necessarily one with all other Christians in his body.

Tell Yourself the Truth

"Community is what Christ is about, and so every believer in Christ is a brother or sister of mine. Also included are past, present, and future believers in Christ. We are all one body. Our common love for the Savior binds us to him, and whoever is bound to him is bound to me as well. I don't concentrate on supposed differences within the body of Christ. They will all fade away in eternity, so why shouldn't they fade away now? I notice that Christians who are persecuted for their faith seem to have more unity than those who face little or no persecution. How foolish to wait until persecution is at the door for us to love one another. I won't wait until that day, should it arrive. I will now speak only good of my brothers and sisters in Christ. I speak unity and love. I will not speak division."

Pray the Promise

Lord, I pray you'd give me a vision of what unity looks like to you. Then I pray I will hold that vision before me as I live with my brothers and sisters here on earth. May your church be one, Lord, just as Jesus prayed.

⌒

"To a true child of God, the invisible bond that unites all believers to Christ is far more tender, and lasting, and precious; and, as we come to recognize and realize that we are all dwelling in one sphere of life in him, we learn to look on every believer as our brother, in a sense that is infinitely higher than all human relationships. This is the one and only way to bring disciples permanently together."

— A. T. PIERSON

God's Strength Is Found in My **Weakness**

The Truth according to God's Word

The LORD turned to him and said, "Go in the strength you have and save Israel out of Midian's hand. Am I not sending you?"

"Pardon me, my lord," Gideon replied, "but how can I save Israel? My clan is the weakest in Manasseh, and I am the least in my family."

The LORD answered, "I will be with you, and you will strike down all the Midianites, leaving none alive." (Judg. 6:14–16)

He gives strength to the weary and increases the power of the weak. (Isa. 40:29)

"Let the weakling say, 'I am strong.'" (Joel 3:10)

He said to me, "My grace is sufficient for you, for my power is made perfect in weakness." Therefore I will boast all the more gladly about my weaknesses, so that Christ's power may rest on me. That is why, for Christ's sake, I delight in weaknesses, in insults, in hardships, in persecutions, in difficulties. For when I am weak, then I am strong. (2 Cor. 12:9–10)

The Truth

Everyone has weaknesses — many of them. Gideon certainly knew about fighting battles with great weakness — and yet God told him to "go in the strength you have." Even the apostle Paul owned up to his weakness. But he knew that it is in weakness that we discover the true strength of God.

Tell Yourself the Truth

"I have many weaknesses. Each weakness, however, reveals the hidden strength of God. Without my weaknesses, how would I discover God's strength? God has allowed these weaknesses for that very reason: He knew I would have to rely on his strength to supplant my weaknesses. Paul gloried in his weaknesses; he wasn't ashamed of them. And I am not ashamed to acknowledge mine. When I do, I am also acknowledging I have found yet another place in my life where God has become my strength."

Pray the Promise

Thank you, Lord, for my many weaknesses. Each one is merely a revelation of where you are going to display your strength next. Thank you that I can depend on your strength when I am weak. Help me remember that when I am weak, I am really strong in you.

∽

"Before he gives strength, we must be made to feel our weakness. Slow, painfully slow, are we to learn this lesson; and slower still to own our nothingness and take the place of helplessness before the Mighty One."

— Arthur W. Pink

God Does Not Hide His **Will.** He Reveals It Day by Day

The Truth according to God's Word

Whether you turn to the right or to the left, your ears will hear a voice behind you, saying, "This is the way; walk in it." (Isa. 30:21)

He who searches our hearts knows the mind of the Spirit, because the Spirit intercedes for God's people in accordance with the will of God. (Rom. 8:27)

Do not conform to the pattern of this world, but be transformed by the renewing of your mind. Then you will be able to test and approve what God's will is — his good, pleasing and perfect will. (Rom. 12:2)

The Truth

Like most everything else in the Christian life, we discern the will of God through faith and compatibility with his Word. If we desire to do his will, we will find ourselves doing it. God doesn't play hide-and-seek with his will. He makes it obvious to those who follow him in faith. Nor is his will hard for us to bear. His will is the pathway to his joy.

Tell Yourself the Truth

"I delight in searching out and doing God's will. I lay down my own will to carry out his will, knowing by experience how unreliable my own will is—and how very reliable is his will. I know that God's way is not burdensome. Rather, God's will is God's reward to us. Happy am I in the middle of God's perfect will. What can harm me there? *Nothing!*"

Pray the Promise

Your will is my will, O Lord. By faith I do the next thing I know to do, only to discover that then I will know the next step to take after that. Your will is therefore revealed step-by-step as I move ahead in faith. May your will be accomplished in my life—your perfect will.

∽

"God is God. Because he is God, he is worthy of my trust and obedience. I will find rest nowhere but in his holy will, a will that is unspeakably beyond my largest notions of what he is up to."

— ELISABETH ELLIOT

God's **Wisdom** Will Lead and Reward Me

The Truth according to God's Word

If any of you lacks wisdom, you should ask God, who gives generously to all without finding fault, and it will be given to you. (James 1:5)

If you are wise, your wisdom will reward you;
if you are a mocker, you alone will suffer. (Prov. 9:12)

Know also that wisdom is like honey for you:
If you find it, there is a future hope for you. (Prov. 24:14)

Be very careful, then, how you live—not as unwise but as wise. (Eph. 5:15)

But the wisdom that comes from heaven is first of all pure; then peace-loving, considerate, submissive, full of mercy and good fruit, impartial and sincere. (James 3:17)

The Truth

There are two kinds of wisdom: earthly wisdom and God's wisdom. God's wisdom, the Bible says, will reward us. Earthly wisdom brings "reward" too. But not a reward that any of us wants. Stick with God's wisdom. Is God's wisdom hard to find? Not according to James. There's just one prerequisite: *ask with a pure motive.*

Tell Yourself the Truth

"My life is a pursuit of God's wisdom, which when I apply it to my life brings great reward. My pursuit leads me to the pages of the Bible, for there the wise mind of God is revealed to me. I ask for wisdom in faith, and God gives it to me. When I act on the wisdom God has given me, things turn out better for me than when I act out of my own weak human wisdom."

Pray the Promise

Lord, you promise a future hope for those who find wisdom; therefore I seek true wisdom. You also say that if I lack wisdom, I should ask and it will be given to me. Then hear me, Lord, now as I do ask. Show me how to be wise concerning the events and relationships in my life. Teach me wisdom from your Word, Lord. I'm listening.

⤷

"Let us make a hearty renunciation of all living apart from Christ, and let us begin from this moment to acknowledge Him in all our ways, and do everything, whatsoever we do, as service to Him and for His glory, depending upon Him alone for wisdom, and strength, and sweetness, and patience, and everything else that is necessary for the right accomplishing of all our living."

— HANNAH WHITALL SMITH

To Be Friends with the **World** Is to Be God's Enemy. I Choose God over This World

The Truth according to God's Word

"What good will it be for someone to gain the whole world, yet forfeit their soul? Or what can anyone give in exchange for their soul?" (Matt. 16:26)

"If the world hates you, keep in mind that it hated me first. If you belonged to the world, it would love you as its own. As it is, you do not belong to the world, but I have chosen you out of the world. That is why the world hates you." (John 15:18 – 19)

Do not conform to the pattern of this world, but be transformed by the renewing of your mind. Then you will be able to test and approve what God's will is — his good, pleasing and perfect will. (Rom. 12:2)

Do not love the world or anything in the world. If anyone loves the world, love for the Father is not in them. For everything in the world — the lust of the flesh, the lust of the eyes, and the pride of life—comes not from the Father but from the world. The world and its desires pass away, but whoever does the will of God lives forever. (1 John 2:15–17)

You, dear children, are from God and have overcome them, because the one who is in you is greater than the one who is in the world. (1 John 4:4)

The Truth

The world as referred to in the New Testament is the mind-set that exalts man's place in the scheme of things and rejects God's plan for man. For many "the world" has a magnetic pull that lures them to think and act in ways that are contrary to God's ways. We are called to be salt in a tasteless world, but sometimes we lose our savory taste and become bland, even preferring the spices of the world to the seasoning of God. That was the situation with the Israelites as they fled from Egypt. They had grown used to the ways of Egypt (a type of the world in the Bible) and longed to return, even though such a return would mean going back into slavery. When we long for the world, we too are forgetting what it was like to be a slave to sin.

As Christians, we need to face the fact that we no longer belong to this world. The kingdom we now belong to is a much superior kingdom in every way. The more we become God's "kingdom people," the less appeal this world will have for us.

Tell Yourself the Truth

"There is a definite 'spirit of the world,' and it has some attraction for me. But I don't go there, knowing that friendship with the world is enmity with God. The tentacles of the world can no longer envelope me, because this world is not my home. I am an alien in a foreign land. While I live in this earthly body, I am in the world but not of the world. And greater is he who is in me than he who is in the world. I'll say it again: *Greater is he who is in me than he who is in the world!*"

Pray the Promise

Father, the world has its attractions, but they pale in comparison to the draw of your kingdom. I resist the world's pull and instead allow your Spirit to draw me further into fellowship with you.

∽

"If you don't feel strong desires for the manifestation of the glory of God, it is not because you have drunk deeply and are satisfied. It is because you have nibbled so long at the table of the world. Your soul is stuffed with small things, and there is no room for the great."

—JOHN PIPER

I Will Not Allow World Events to Cause Me to Fear

The Truth according to God's Word

Jesus answered: "Watch out that no one deceives you. For many will come in my name, claiming, 'I am the Messiah,' and will deceive many. You will hear of wars and rumors of wars, but see to it that you are not alarmed. Such things must happen, but the end is still to come. Nation will rise against nation, and kingdom against kingdom. There will be famines and earthquakes in various places. All these are the beginning of birth pains." (Matt. 24:4–8)

"Be always on the watch, and pray that you may be able to escape all that is about to happen, and that you may be able to stand before the Son of Man." (Luke 21:36)

The Truth

Debt crisis, terrorism, earthquakes, wars, floods, home invasions, and more are all a part of the world events we read about daily. And the Bible teaches that there will come a time when world events become catastrophic. Jesus asks of such a time, "When the

Son of Man comes, will he find faith on the earth?" Yes, he will. We will be faithful to him.

Tell Yourself the Truth

"No one knows the future, except God. The day and hour of Christ's return cannot be known by man. Jesus did point to some signs of his coming though. Signs that some say are happening now. But I don't fear world events whether Christ returns in my lifetime or after I'm gone. Either way, God has the veto power over any madness that Satan tries to unleash on earth.

"I believe that in the face of coming world events, God will raise up a strong presence among his people. He will always have a people through whom he can show his mercy, a people who will be a witness to his promise that he is not willing that any should perish but that all should come to repentance.

"By God's grace, I will be among those faithful. I will stand in the face of the world's coming troubles. I will stand not in my own strength—that would be sheer foolishness—but I will stand by his power. More and more, I give my life over to him to work through me, weaknesses and all. And more and more, God honors that prayer and plants courage in my heart.

"Maranatha. Come soon, Lord!"

Pray the Promise

I am not scared, Lord, about the future. I know that as events unfold, I may be tempted to fear, but I must always remind myself that your Word gave us these warnings so we could be prepared. Each nerve-rattling world event just means we're that much closer to your coming.

"God has wisely kept us in the dark concerning future events and reserved for himself the knowledge of them, that he may train us up in a dependence upon himself and a continued readiness for every event."

— MATTHEW HENRY

I Lay Down My **Worries** and Pick Up God's Peace

The Truth according to God's Word

Cast your cares on the LORD
    and he will sustain you;
    he will never let
    the righteous be shaken. (Ps. 55:22)

Truly he is my rock and my salvation;
    he is my fortress, I will not be shaken. (Ps. 62:6)

They will have no fear of bad news;
    their hearts are steadfast, trusting in the LORD. (Ps. 112:7)

"Therefore I tell you, do not worry about your life, what you will eat or drink; or about your body, what you will wear. Is not life more than food, and the body more than clothes? Look at the birds of the air; they do not sow or reap or store away in barns, and yet your heavenly Father feeds them. Are you not much more valuable than they? Can any one of you by worrying add a single hour to your life?" (Matt. 6:25–27)

"Do not let your hearts be troubled. You believe in God; believe also in me." (John 14:1)

Do not be anxious about anything, but in every situation, by prayer and petition, with thanksgiving, present your requests to

God. And the peace of God, which transcends all understanding, will guard your hearts and your minds in Christ Jesus. (Phil. 4:6–7)

The Truth

Worry comes from assuming responsibilities God never intended us to have. It's a signal that it's time to turn the matter over to God. It can also be a needless preoccupation over a future event, possibly one over which we have no control. When we acknowledge that God is in charge, we can cease worrying. Sure, it may take practice not worrying, but with the promises of God on our lips, we can end our worry habit sooner.

Tell Yourself the Truth

"The moment worry creeps into my mind, I will immediately resist the thought and turn my attention to God and his power over my situation. I exchange worry for praise, knowing that God has taken care of my situation."

Pray the Promise

Lord, you take my worries and replace them with your peace. I resign each worry to your care, and I rest easy. No worry is too small for you to receive and no worry is too big for you to handle.

↭

"Worry does not empty tomorrow of its sorrow. It empties today of its strength."

— CORRIE TEN BOOM

God Places Zeal in My Heart and Tempers It over Time So That It Burns Long and Strong

The Truth according to God's Word

Never be lacking in zeal, but keep your spiritual fervor, serving the Lord. (Rom. 12:11)

[Jesus] gave Himself for us, that He might redeem us from every lawless deed and purify for Himself His own special people, zealous for good works. (Titus 2:14 NKJV)

The Truth

Zeal is God's enthusiasm coursing through our inner being, working its way out to good deeds.

Tell Yourself the Truth

"I don't lack in zeal, but keep my spiritual fervor as I serve the Lord. When my embers start to burn low, I pray that the soft wind of the Holy Spirit will fan my zeal back to full passionate fire. May the zeal of the Lord be among us all."

Pray the Promise

Stoke my fire, Lord. Make me ablaze for you!

⤳

"Spirit-filled souls are ablaze for God. They love with a love that glows. They serve with a faith that kindles. They serve with a devotion that consumes. They hate sin with fierceness that burns. They rejoice with a joy that radiates. Love is perfected in the fire of God. Let no man join us who is afraid, and we want none but those who are saved, sanctified, and aflame with the fire of the Holy Spirit."

— SAMUEL CHADWICK

One Final Exercise

As you close this book, I hope you're convinced that the promises of God are for *you*. I hope in the years ahead, you'll always make God's Word your anchor.

All of us have different troubling issues we face, so here's a brief assignment to get you started in personalizing the promises of God to meet your particular need. On pages 318–19 you'll find two blank setups for you to fill in based on some possible needs you might have from the list that follows. I've supplied the headlines. You fill in the rest.

But first, here are a couple of thoughts to get you going:

- Don't be locked into just one Bible translation. Some Bible versions are clearer than others when speaking to a particular topic. For one situation you might prefer the English Standard Version. For another, it might be the New International Version, the New King James Version, or even a paraphrase such as *The Message*.

- To find the pertinent verses on a topic, you can use a concordance or topical Bible. The former lists the words in the Bible and where they're found, so make sure you're using a concordance for the translation you're using. A topical Bible lists many of the topics in the Bible. A good Internet resource is Biblegateway.com. It has a search field for topics. Also, as you read your Bible daily, use a highlighter to mark verses that strike you as promises for your needs.

The following topics are just suggestions. If none seem appropriate, you can simply identify your needs yourself.

"The Childhood Abuse I Suffered Does Not Define Me."
"Divorce Hurts, but I Will Recover."
"I Am Part of Christ's Body, the Church."
"I Will Get Past This Painful Memory of That Horrible Event."
"Being Bipolar Will Not Destroy My Future."
"God Knows about My Post-Traumatic Distress Disorder and Cares."
"I Serve My Country Proudly in the Military."
"I Will Not Allow This Root of Bitterness to Plague Me."
"I Pray and Believe God Will Bring Revival to This Land."
"God Is My Friend — My Best Friend."
"My Loved One Died, but God Will Help Me Go On."
"My Pride Gives Way to Humility When I Think of Christ."
"School Is a Challenge, but God Will Help Me Make It Through."
"I Will Be Healed from the Memory of My Abortion."
"God Will Show Me How to Move On from This Loss and Betrayal."
"God Gives Me Traveling Mercies."
"God Has the Solution to My Panic Attacks."
"God Is with Me When I'm Confronted by a Bully."
"God Has Called Me to Be a Good Husband."
"God Has Called Me to Be a Good Wife."
"I Do Not Envy Others; Neither Am I Jealous."
"Thank God, His Mercy Is Never-Ending."
"God Will Help Me with My ADHD and/or ADD."

My prayer is that every reader of *Power in the Promises* will become an expert in relying on God's wonderful promises. Remember that practice makes perfect. Start today trusting God to keep his promises and keep it up for the rest of your life. May his joy be yours as you do!

Nick

Topic:

The Truth according to God's Word

Verse 1:

Verse 2:

(Add additional verses as appropriate.)

The Truth

Tell Yourself the Truth

Pray the Promise

Topic:

The Truth according to God's Word

Verse 1:

Verse 2:

(Add additional verses as appropriate.)

The Truth

Tell Yourself the Truth

Pray the Promise

Magnificent Prayer

366 Devotions to Deepen Your Prayer Experience

Nick Harrison

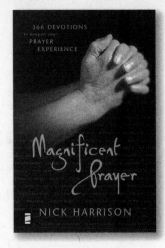

Have you ever sensed that you've seen just the foothills of what prayer is all about? Do you long for more? *Magnificent Prayer* points you toward the heights of communion with God. Drawing insights from classic and contemporary pioneers of prayer, Nick Harrison guides you on a yearlong devotional course of discovery, application, and growth.

> *It is a vibrant resource for your spiritual walk. Day by day, your prayers will be enhanced as you live in close communication with your true and faithful Guide. I recommend this volume without reservation. You will be blessed by this book.*
>
> —Anne Graham Lotz

> *I love this book. It beautifully captures the heart and soul of prayer. A book worthy of the name "Magnificent."*
>
> —Liz Curtis Higgs

> *A deep and satisfying reservoir of spiritual replenishment.*
>
> —Lee Strobel

> *One of my all-time favorite books. Just a short reading a day can be the beginning of a whole new era in your walk with God.*
>
> —Mark Mittelberg

> *Almost every day, in my own daily devotions, I read* Magnificent Prayer.
>
> —Jim Cymbala

> *God has used* Magnificent Prayer *to teach, motivate, and inspire me ... greatly over the years.*
>
> —Chip Ingram

Available in stores and online!

His Victorious Indwelling

Daily Devotions for a Deeper Christian Life

Nick Harrison, Editor

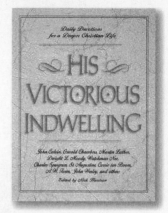

Have you truly grasped the remarkable heritage that is yours in Christ? Through the years, certain Christians have stood out for their deep insight into the riches we possess in Christ: Oswald Chambers, A. W. Tozer, Hannah Whittal Smith, D. L. Moody, E. M. Bounds—these men and women knew the secrets of the abundant spiritual life. Drawing on the meditations and quotes from these and other well-known writers, *His Victorious Indwelling* explores Christ's victory and how it can be lived through us.

> His Victorious Indwelling *will be treasured by the church for a long time to come.*
>
> —Miles Stanford

> *I have used devotionals regularly for 20+ years but have not yet found one that compares to this gem. I highly recommend every page of this devotional.*
>
> —E.N. on Amazon.com

> *After three decades of devotional reading, I found 72 of my favorite authors in this gem of a devotional book, plus dozens of others. Sincere thanks to Mr. Harrison and to Zondervan.*
>
> —K.J. on Amazon.com

> *I would recommend this to anyone who hungers for more of Jesus!*
>
> —J.S. on Amazon.com

> *This book is my favorite devotional ever! I have bought about 100 copies in the past five or so years to give to people as gifts. It has been so instrumental in my walk with Christ.*
>
> —D.G. on Amazon.com

> *I have read this through for two years now and it never fails to encourage, inspire, challenge, or convict me. One of my all-time favorites.*
>
> —J.Z. on Amazon.com

Available in stores and online!

ZONDERVAN®
.com

Author photo by Jay Eads

Nick Harrison is a writer and editor based in the Pacific Northwest where he lives with his wife, Beverly. They are the parents of three adult children and the grandparents of four. Nick's previous books include *Magnificent Prayer* and *His Victorious Indwelling*. His website and blog can be found at nickharrisonbooks.com.